This book is dedicated to all the teachers in my life.
May it inspire you as they have inspired me.

2019 Music Industry Success
Publicity
Marketing
Touring
Album Release

www.JosiahGarrett.com
2019 Copyright Josiah Garrett

Letter from the author

This book is a practical guide to 4 important modules of the music industry – Publicity, Marketing, Touring, and Album Release. This book is not in any sort of chronological order, its more of a "choose-your-own-adventure" book. Pick and choose whichever chapter you want and read at whatever pace you please. Each chapter is, for the most part, a standalone article on that topic. And each module features topics that are in a similar category.

This book contains niche ideas as well as general knowledge, and is based off of my years of experiences in the Music Industry. Also, I should note that this book focuses on the practices of the United States, so please take that into consideration if you live internationally.

And, lastly, finally, thirdly, ultimately....
This book is only one persons account of an enormous and complicated world. This book will not walk you through every obstacle in the industry or your musical career. The best way to learn is to learn by doing. So go out there and start doing :)

Hopefully this helps.
~Josiah Garrett

Table Of Contents

PUBLICITY & PR

The Website
The Electronic Press Kit
Publicity Outlets
Press Release Checklist

The Website

"Is your website functional and compelling enough to keep a fan's interest in your brand?"

A Band's website is the hub of their musical activity. By directing your fans back to your website, you make deeper connections yes, but more importantly you are in complete control of your fan's experience with your brand. Your website can act as your Landing Page for your band's marketing and should be the One-Stop-Shop for fans to find anything they need to know about you.

The Rules for Your Website

RULE #1: Gather Data
  - *Who is your audience?*
  - *Where do they come from?*
  - *What do they want?*
  - *How do they interact with your site?*
  - *Am I keeping track of my analytics?*
  - *Have I refined my message to my target audience?*

RULE #2: Have a Strong Front Page
You have less than 10 seconds to convince a new fan; Grab 'em while you can!

RULE #3: Keep it Simple
Save creativity for the blog posts and social media content!

RULE #4: Keep it Updated
An out of date website is a huge turnoff for fans and industry professionals alike, keep your site updated with recent news and content!

RULE #5: Make it Personal
Fans are there to hear from you!

RULE #6: Create a Community
Your website is your hub for online presence. Creating call to action buttons, social media links, and a newsletter sign-up on your homepage is a good place to start.

Website Analytics

You need to be gathering Analytics about your audience as they visit your website. Google Analytics and Facebook both offer platforms for tracking your audience and their interaction with your website.

By gathering analytics, you will be able to answer questions like:
- *Where is my audience coming from?*
- *What Keywords are they using to search?*
- *What drove my audience to my website?*
- *How long does my audience look at each page on my website?*
- *What is the Age range, location of my audience?*
- *Does my actual audience meet the expectations of my target audience?*

When you collect and measure your analytics, you can:
- Fine tune the efficiency of your website
- Gain Keyword insight to improve your SEO
- Track and React to Trends in Real Time
- More efficiently allocate time and money across your sales channels
- Assess and Improve your Bounce Rate (*Your* **Bounce Rate** *is the percentage of people that leave your website after visiting only 1 page*)

Free Analytics platforms:
- Google Analytics
- Facebook Pixel

The EPK (Electronic Press Kit)

A very important page on the website of a young band is the Electronic Press Kit, or *EPK*; this page is the gateway to getting booked at new venues and doing DIY Publicity. You will have the most success creating the EPK as an "invisible" page on your website, a page that is unable to be navigated to on the website unless you have the URL. That way you can tailor the content on this page for Venues and Promoters and you won't have to worry about your fans stumbling onto it.

It is important that your EPK be hosted on your website and not formatted or included in an email. At the time of this writing, the standard inbox size is 15GB. So if you send an email to 20 promoters hoping to book a tour and you attach 10 songs and 5 Hi-Res photos, you are occupying an important 100mb of space in that Promoters email Inbox. It is considered courteous to include as few attachments as possible and instead include hyper-links in the body of the email.

With so much potential content for an EPK it can be hard to create something that is both well organized and visually appealing, but here are some helpful tips to help you highlight your strengths:

Highlight your Strengths

1. Gather quotes from reviews, venues, or fans and add the best ones to your page
2. Prepare Long and Short bio options. This allows for a quick grab, read, or copy for bloggers that need information about you quickly.
3. Make Use of your Music! Assemble a few of your best performances and incorporate them as the focal point of your EPK. Keep this music player compact, such as an embedded Spotify player embed. Remember, in this day and age "Your Music is your Marketing"

Photos
Add images that are full-resolution for bloggers and Social Media posts. These photos should be pre-cropped to the correct ratios of different platforms: Portrait, Landscape (16 x 9) and Square. Your responsibility is to make it as easy as possible for bloggers to repost your content to their audience. Posed photos and Live shots are both important to have.

The more photo variation, the better. Also, don't forget to include multiple file types for your Logo – a transparent PNG image being the most important.

Videos

Add videos (links) to promote what your band looks and sounds like, such as music videos, live videos, or promotional videos. High Quality Audio on the videos is very important, for obvious reasons!

Layout

Keeping your EPK section uncluttered is as important as having all the ingredients. Assume you have a 10–15 second window of capturing the attention of a new visitor. Make use of columns and feature titles, as well as color contrast in your design. Contact Information is the most important message, so make sure people who visit your EPK know how to get in touch with you! Include phone numbers and email addresses for your manager, booking agent, label and Publicist, as well as links to your social media and even a contact form.

How to Build Credibility

The *baseline* is the crucial information about the band or artist, such as a bio and contact information. More importantly, it is an affirmation of the band or artist as business minded, long–term goal oriented and diligent. Even if some of this information is never used, the process of assembling and maintaining this information establishes "baseline" credibility for your band when moving forward in the Publicity / PR side of the music business.

- Main Contact Home Address; individual addresses.
- Main Contact Phone number, individual phone numbers.
- Main Contact Email Address; individual address.
- Name and short bio of each member of the band
- 4–6 Sentence Band bio (written by the client)
- 30 Second Sales–Pitch
- Mission Statement
- Website URL
- High Quality Picture of the band
- High Quality audio recordings – Physical

- High Quality audio recordings and links – Digital
- Previous and Upcoming Tour Dates
- RIYL – Recommended If You Like
- Any and all existing press: Reviews, Interviews, Quotes, etc
- Promo Videos
- Discography with Links
- Stage Plot
- Links to All Existing Social Media

Cover Letter:
- *"What is our Mission Statement"*
- *"What is our Sales Pitch?"*
- *"What do we bring to the table?"*
- *"How are we unique?"*
- *"What makes us more desirable to our fan base than others?"*

Artist Biography:
- Be between 4–6 sentences.
- Include enough factual information about the band to be the main content of an article, expose, feature, or review
- Be written in 3rd person
- *"Create a narrative that both gives the reader an interesting and captivating glimpse of your influences, uniqueness, and other aspects that comprise your artistry; and most of all, makes then want to experience what you have to offer"*

Publicity Outlets

As a general rule, *"3rd party endorsements are by far more powerful than anything you can say about yourself and your work"*, which is why brands are so hungry for publicity. Establishing relationships with publicity outlets, or PO's, is the bread and butter of any good publicist or promotional team. Your relationship with these PO's is as important as the content you are promoting, so be diligent in building your network.

Publicity Outlet is a broad term, but essentially it is some form of media that can distribute information about a product, person, or company for promotional reasons. In order to talk about the types of PO's, we can place them on a scale based on their content consumption.

1. Audio-centric content tends to be passive consumption.
2. Printed outlets are the most active consumption of content
3. Digital is somewhere in between.

Print Outlets
- Event Calendars
- Newspaper
- Magazines
- Flyers
- Posters
- Billboards (Automated + digital billboards. These are good for longer commutes and brand awareness)

Digital Outlets
- Social Media
- Influencer Pages
- Online Magazine
- Online Newspapers
- Blogs
- Video Streaming services (Twitch, YouTube, Facebook Watch, IG TV)

Audio Outlets
  - College and Non-Commercial Radio
  - Online Radio
  - Satellite Radio
  - Podcasts
  - Public Playlists

From here you have 2 paths. You can either
1. Hire a Publicist
2. Do It Yourself

The Publicist

A Publicist is someone who arranges press coverage, such as album reviews, concert reviews, features, video premieres, and in-person appearances. Your publicist will exclusively arrange radio, tv and magazine interviews, but can coordinate their work with a team when it comes to album coverage. Publicists are generally hired in terms of 3-6 months and are paid a monthly fee over the course of the campaign. If you decide to work with a publicist, make sure that you clearly express your goals for the publicity campaign and bear in mind that there is no such thing as a sure-fire PR campaign. Just like selling tickets, you are at the mercy of the market, except the currency in the PR market is attention.

If you decide to be your own publicist (which I call DIY Publicity), you might be asking yourself *"Where Do I Start?"*

The 3 Steps to DIY Publicity

Step 1. Collect
Collect various contact points from digital, print, and audio related publicity outlets
  - Music News Media
  - Online Radio/Streams
  - Podcasts
  - Playlists
  - College Radio
  - Blogs

- Facebook pages and other social media accounts
- Music Entertainment Media
- Music Magazines
- Music Event Calendars
- Local Publications + Bi-Weeklies

Step 2: Prepare
Prepare personalized Press Releases for individual outlet types
- Physical Press Release
- Digital Press Release
- Radio Feature Request
- Feature Request
- Audio Release
- Booking Inquiry
- One Sheet

Step 3: Send
Send personalized emails or letters to your contacts.
- YOU HAVE TO SEND THEM!

Tips for DIY Publicity
– Expect a 5–10% response rate
– Follow up with every response
– Be friendly
– You should never have to pay for publicity. (*That is called advertising and we will talk about paid content placement in greater detail in another chapter*)

Things to Avoid In PR and Publicity
These are things that either violate the mutual respect between a publicist and a publicity outlet, or will leave your recipients questioning the professionalism of your work.

1. Avoid Sending unsolicited Press Kits unless otherwise noted

2. Avoid Sending Press material to Editors and Directors! They have enough on their plates. Most creative work or essay writing is done by interns, creative directors, authors, or freelance writers.

3. Avoid using incorrect grammar, abbreviations, slang, and casual diction. If writing to a new outlet for the first time, for example, head your message "Hello Mr. Bond", not "hey James"

4. Don't forget to Proofread!

5. Cool is never declared. Your job as a publicist is not to write persuasive papers but to present factual and relevant information and let the receiver make of your presentation how they will.

Press Release Checklist

Press Release – Music news media outlets (Physical and Digital), Music Blogs
Audio Release – Online Streams, Playlists
Radio Feature Request – College Radio Stations, Podcasts, Online Radio
Booking Inquiry – Music Venues, Festivals, Events, Booking and Management Agencies
One Sheet – Condenses all aspects of a Press Kit into one page

Physical Press Release:

Recipients: Editors and Writers at Newspapers, Bi-Weeklies, Music Magazines
  - Physical CD/Demo
  - One Sheet
  - Cover Letter
  - Artist Biography
  - High Quality Picture of the Band
  - Previous and Upcoming Tour Dates
  - Any and All Press Contact Information – Website URL
  - Discography

Digital Press Release:

Recipients: Editors and Contributors to Online Magazines, Blogs, Digital Media Outlets
  - One Sheet
  - Links to High Quality Audio Recordings
  - Link to Discography
  - Link to Social Media
  - High Quality Picture of the Band or Artist
  - Any and All Press
  - Video Promotion
  - RIYL
  - Cover Letter
  - Artist Biography
  - Previous and Upcoming Tour Dates
  - Contact Information – Website URL

Feature Request:

Recipients: Editors and Writers at Large Magazines and Digital Blogs, & YouTube Channels
  - One Sheet
  - Links to High Quality Audio Recordings
  - Link to Discography and Website
  - Link to Social Media
  - Cover Letter
  - RIYL
  - Previous and Upcoming Tour Dates
  - Any and All Press
  - Video Promotion
  - Artist Biography
  - Contact Information

Audio Release:

Recipients: Music Directors and DJ's at Radio Stations (College Radio, Non-Commercial Radio, Satellite Radio), Playlist Curators, & YouTube channels
  - One Sheet
  - Links to High Quality Audio Recordings
  - Links to Discography and Website
  - RIYL
  - Artist Biography
  - Any and All Press
  - Contact Information

Booking Inquiry Checklist:

Recipients: Talent Agencies, Booking Agencies, & Music Festival Talent Buyers
  - Physical CD/Demo
  - Discography
  - RIYL
  - Stage Plot
  - Ticket Sales

One Sheet:

Condenses all the aspects of a Press Kit into a single page, typically used for an album release.

Recipients: All (Venues, Booking Agents, Private clients, Music Retailers, Magazine editors, Music Directors, Radio Station DJ's, & Management Companies

- Bio/Mission Statement
- Pitch
- CD Art and Track List
- Photos
- Contact Information
- Upcoming Performances
- 3rd Party Quotes

MARKETING

Building A Brand

"A promise of quality and consistency"

Brand is defined as the emotional attachment the consumer associates with your business such as a customer's overall perception of your business and the intangible sum of the attributes of your products. Simply put, a **brand** is a promise of quality and consistency.

Here are some Examples of great Brands:
 - **Vimeo** rose to compete against YouTube by focusing on professional videographers, and emphasizing hi-resolution streaming and embedding techniques.
 - **Netflix** destroyed Blockbuster on the promise of never running out of stock on hard to find cult classics and established a consumer experience where by they didn't even need to leave the house.
 - **Tesla** challenged the Prius as the leading hybrid car on the market by marketing to high-end, luxury automobile owners.
 - **Amazon** emphasized the customer's experience over anything else in their business. Amazon dominated the young eCommerce market with customer satisfaction techniques such as their patented Single-Click Purchase. They seized the under-priced opportunity of search engine advertising in the late 90's and exploded into the largest company that has ever existed.

These companies researched the market where they had competition, found an available space in consumer perception of their competition, and built a promise of quality and consistency. In doing so, they built their brand and took their businesses to the next level.

To make money as a musician, or group of musicians, you have to sell something. And unfortunately, the Era of selling your music ended with the birth of the iPod, so you gotta sell something else. It's 2019 now, and it's time to realize that your music is your marketing, not your product. The next generation of consumer is an experience driven consumer base. They aren't as interested in the tangible as much as they were in the 90's. That's why so many businesses are shutting their doors - Toys R Us, Blockbuster, Brookstone, Mattress Firm, Sears, KMart, Barnes and Noble... Retail Businesses as we know them are dying.

You need to be building your business to be successful in 2025, not in 2018. You need to sell the experience of music. But first, you need to build a Brand.

Ask Yourself:
- *Who are you?*
- *Where have you come from?*
- *Where are you going?*
- *What is your musical direction?*
- *What do you stand for and why?*
- *What makes you different or unique?*

Your Brand Must:
- Portray your music and your personality
- Be kept simple and honest
- Differentiate yourself
- Maintain a consistent look
- Have a remarkable logo
- Have great photos
- Give Value

11 Steps Towards Building a Better Brand

Step 1: Determine your brand's target audience
Keep in mind who you are trying to reach and tailor your message to them.

Step 2: Define your Mission Statement
This should reflect your message, personality, logo, passions, and goals as a business.

Step 3: Research Brands within your Industry
- Be aware of what they do well and what they don't.
- Use this knowledge to differentiate yourselves from them
- Outline the key qualities and benefits that your brand offers over others and that make you unique

Step 4: Create a remarkable Logo and tagline
Your logo is the gateway into your brand, so be willing to invest time and money into this

Step 5: Form your brand's business voice
A business voice is how you communicate with your customers. Choose a voice that resonated with your target audience:
- Professional
- Friendly
- Service-Oriented
- Promotional
- Conversational
- Informative

Step 6: Build a brand message
A brand message is an opportunity to communicate with your target audience on a human level. Use this opportunity to make a direct emotional connection with your fan-base

Step 7: Build an Elevator Pitch
Elevator Pitch: A simple and clear answer to the question "Why is your brand important?"
- No more than 1-2 sentences

Step 8: Integrate your brand into every aspect of your business
- Business cards
- Advertisements
- Social media
- Website Design
- Logo
- Color Scheme
- Tour Poster

Step 9: Stay true to your brand!
Consistency is key

Step 10: Be your brand's biggest advocate
When seeking to expand your team, encourage them to align with the mission, vision, and values of your brand

Step 11: If you Don't Love it, Don't Do it!
If you don't love your product or service, then it isn't worth your time. And if that's the case you should find something that you love and do that. Because this is going to be the hardest thing you've ever done.

Email Marketing & Newsletters

Your audience is the most precious resource for an emerging artist. Creating promotional efforts directed at them warms up your audience and encourages a more dedicated fan-base. Email marketing campaigns, typically in the form of a newsletter, are sent out to their fans through a **List-Serve**, which is an electronic mailing list, via a third party application.

You should look for a Mailing List service that offers:
- Free Option
- Custom Press Releases and Newsletter with powerful editing features
- Real Time Analytics such as Open and Click Through Rates

5 Steps for Powerful Email Engagement
1: Assemble a Database
2: Create a Schedule
3: Design the Email
4: Test It
5: Study the Analytics

Step 1: Assemble a Database
Every band or artist attempts to gather their fans information at shows, usually on an unorganized sign-up sheet somewhere on the merch table. But with little incentive for fans to give their information or, more importantly, interact with your brand, it is no wonder that your database of potential customers is tucked away in the back of the merch box to never see the light of day. When someone walks up to your merch table, that is a pivotal engagement between you and a potential customer! If they have taken the time to approach your pop-up shop of shirts, lighters and stickers it is because they are interested in your brand. And so you need to make it as easy as possible for your fans to give you their information and connect with you.

Your Database should include whatever kind of information you want from your audience, but traditional email marketing emphasizes Name, email, and city/state of residence or zipcode. I also like to include the Date and venue, and you can write this in yourself when you pack up your merch table. This is so you can send very targeted emails announcing shows or events to a segment of your audience. It is a good idea to consolidate all of your contacts into an organized and accessible digital spreadsheet and update it frequently. If an email address bounced back, take it off the list. If your database is digital, in a place like Google Sheets, it can managed by multiple members of the band and easily accessed by your publicist.

Step 2: Create a Schedule

Typically your Newsletter should correspond to the timeline of an important event. This includes Tour Dates, an Album Release, or a special show. If you can plan out a detailed release schedule in 3 to 6 months in advance, coordinating your email marketing efforts will be much easier. It will also make assembling the necessary content for the email marketing much easier, such as press photos, tour ad mats, posters, album artwork, audio embed links, promo videos, banners, etc.

You should regularly update you listserv and send a welcome email to new subscribers within 14 days of them signing up. The first email, as long as your email account hasn't been flagged as spam by Google (which definitely will happen if you buy email lists so don't do that), will go into their Primary inbox. Use this to point fans towards your landing page, social media pages, facebook groups, or website. (Whatever you want) Unlike most of your brand's digital interactions the welcome email should be very personal. Talk about the show, or the city, or the venue, or the food you ate. If you recorded the show, offer them an mp3 of it for their listening enjoyment. Maybe include a setlist. Make them feel like you are sending this email just for them. Which, you are.

Step 3: Design the Email

This is the fun part! The visuals, design, layout, and other creative elements are completely up to you. Mailchimp, as well as most other email marketing platforms, have hundreds of templates and designs to get you started right away. Other than a few crucial elements that shouldn't be overlooked, your newsletter design is entirely your own. Ultimately, your newsletter should look professional and uncluttered, and should prominently feature your band's logo and photographs. It needs to highlight a central message and have purpose. But most importantly, it

Step 4: Test It

This is so important! There are few things that says "unprofessional" as much as sending a redacted or edited newsletter out to contacts because the initial send was not:
- Proofread
- Checked for link-compatibility
- Sent to a focus group
- Containing Up-to-date Information

Testing your newsletter to a few trusted sources before sending to the masses will save you and your band a massive headache if something has indeed been overlooked.

Step 5: Study the Analytics

Most email newsletter platforms, such as Mailchimp, allow you to easily embed email sign-up forms directly onto you website. And vice versa, Most websites platforms, like Wix, Squarespace, Wordpress, and Shopify have simple integration tools for email sign-up forms. Additionally, you can make use of "*Auto-Responders*". When people sign up for the email list on your website, an Auto-Responder will send an initial email thanking them for signing up, visiting the website, or purchasing something from the store. This is a good medium for offers, like a permanent 10% off "valued customer" coupon, or for a funnel towards your bands' social media accounts.

These email marketing platforms come with tools to measure and report your marketing efficiency and functionality, such as statistics that measure "open rate", "click-through rate", "unsubscriber rate", and much more. Studying these analytics will help you craft better email marketing campaigns and can assist you when assembling progress reports, business plans, market research, or new member of your press team.

Email Marketing Essentials:

Don't spam!
- Ensure that everyone on your mailing list has actually signed up for it.

Don't over-communicate
- Leave decent gaps of time between your emails. Save email marketing campaigns for big announcements, like tour dates or an album release

Stay on Topic
- Always send relevant, interesting content to the your mailing list to minimize your unsubscriber rate.

Make it easy for people to unsubscriber
- It should take 1 click

Adhere to data protection laws.
- You might want to look those up if you have any questions.

20 Words to avoid in your Email Subject Line
(Unless you want to go straight into the Spam/Promotions tab:)

- Free
- Available now
- Download
- Discount
- Guarantee
- Sign up now
- Offer
- Win
- Order now
- Hundreds
- Thousands
- Millions
- Share
- Deal
- Announced
- Sale
- Coupon
- Savings
- Release
- ANY WORD IN ALL CAPS

High-Quality Content

"Strike emotion to capture attention"

The content that you create for your brand can be divided into 2 categories: *Micro* Content and *Macro* Content.

Micro Content: Short Form/Low Cost
- Photos
- Videos less than 60 seconds
- Text
- Most Social Media Posts

Macro Content: Long Form/High Cost
- Blog Posts
- Photo Galleries
- YouTube Videos
- Documentaries
- Podcasts
- Live Streams

How To Create High-Quality Content:

Give More than You Take
The currency of marketing is attention. Every piece of content you show to your audience is your brand asking your audience to pay attention. The reason our attention spans have shortened is because we are asked to give our attention so much more often today than we were 5, 10, 20 years ago. We are much more easily able to determine what content is valuable and relevant to us. Don't waste your audiences time, because that mean you are wasting their currency – The currency is attention.

Originality
As Neil Patel says, *"If you don't have anything original to say then don't say anything at all."*
- Be unique in the content that you create
- Always be on the offense
- Change the rules that the game is played

Strong Headlines

Statistically, 8 out of 10 people will read your headline, but only 2 out of 10 will engage with the rest of the content. The title of your content holds a disproportionate amount of power over the content itself in terms of audience engagement. I recommend creating a few titles for each piece of content and then choosing the best one.

Provide Answers

When people use a search engine, it is because they need an answer to a question. Its a similar consumer experience when they read a blog post or watch a video.

Be Accurate

If you are going to evoke statistics, facts, or quotes, make sure that they are accurate and can be verified. Your content is a reflection of your brand and maintaining trust with your audience is paramount.

Provoke Thought and Interest

The only way to engage an audience is to make engaging content. Pay extra attention to your copy, introduction, and storytelling.

Get to the Point

A longer piece of content does not mean a better piece of content. If you actively work to eliminate fluff and non-essential content, it'll make the piece as a whole much easier for consumption.

Creative Content for 2019

- Blog Posts
- Podcasting *
- AMA's (Which stands for Ask Me Anything) **
- Live Streams
- Snapchat and IG Stories

Podcasting

Content creation as a whole is moving towards passive consumption. Podcasting can be a great way to share your story or your knowledge with the world. And since podcasts are free, you can record and upload a podcast with very little overhead.

For example, I have recorded this entire book in audio format and uploaded it as the first 22 episodes of my debut podcast, A Modern Music Industry. Podcasting can be as simple as recycling the audio content that you are already creating, or it can be a stand-alone content format. Such as: Interviewing your friends, doing a producer/ artist commentary on songs that you release, or simply telling a narrative about your life. Podcasting is a way of "lifting the veil", and should give an honest look into your life or musical jounrey.

AMA: Ask Me Anything

These are very popular because they work! An AMA stems from the popular Forum website, Reddit, which is a self-maintained and moderated community of people from around the world. You can use the AMA format on a variety of social mediums, such as facebook video post, youTube live stream, periscope, facebook live, IG Live, and of course Reddit. Doing an AMA gives your fan-base the opportunity to ask any question that they want and engage with the band in a friendly, quiet, non-performance related environment. It improves your relationship with your consumer and that is so important for the long run. If you have an existing fan base, definitely consider hosting a few AMA's a year as a way to connect to your community.

Social Media

Social Media is a massive sphere of "Word of Mouth", and word-of-mouth is considered to be the most trusted source of information. If you can convince people to speak highly about your product or service to others, your influence as a brand will grow exponentially.

The currency of Social Media is Attention
- *What does your audience want?*
- *What are you selling?*
- *Do you have leverage?*

How To Create High Quality Social Media:

- Give more than you take
- Create Objectively High Quality Content
- Hi-Definition videos
- Good Audio Quality
- Closed Captioning
- Media Encoding
- Keyword Optimization
- Getting to the point
  If you spend 20 seconds on a 2 minute youTube video introducing yourself, then you have certainly lost my attention
- Play the Long Game
- Don't just sell a product, build a community

Impressions are good, Engagement is great, but Conversion is King. You either convert, or you don't. You either sell tickets, or you don't. You either make a living doing what you love, or you don't.

Components of A Social Media Campaign

Social media campaigns are comprised of 3 components:
> *Content*
> *Mediums*
> *Intent*

Content

Video, Song, Album, Vinyl pre-order, New Merch, Patiently crafted picture, blog post, album review, a new podcast, a sponsorship for your event, an important announcement, A new Website. YouTube, Blog, Mailing List, Music Files on an online hosting site

Mediums

(These go by many names, Gary Vaynerchuk calls them Platforms, Grant Cardone calls them Channels) Facebook, Twitter, Instagram, Pinterest, the comments section of YouTube, Live Streaming platform like Twitch TV or Periscope, Musically, Snapchat, Tik Tok, RIP Vine Compilations, an in-person meet and greet. Virtual Reality is just around the corner. Interaction is any platform in which you can interact, preferably in real time, with your audience on social media.

Intent

What is the purpose of the content and the social medium? Why are you posting content to social media? What do you want and did you get it? This is the most overlooked component of good social media management. You will produce better content over time if the purpose of your social media campaigns are measurable.

(I want this video to get X many views) or (I want this event to be seen by X many people) or (I want to hear feedback about our new album from X many listeners)

Are you trying to push your audience to a landing page?
To buy a product?
To increase Engagement or Branding?
To promote something specific?

Its OK if most of your social media posts are measured for branding or engagement. And in a lot of ways, it is impossible to measure much of the results of a social media campaign. You really just need to make sure that your content matches your interaction platform, and that your performance goals are being worked towards.

Social Media Metrics that Matter

Social media campaigns are analyzed and measured with 3 metrics:
Awareness
Interaction
Conversion

Awareness

Impression: is the number of times a piece of content is viewed once by a visitor.

Reach: refers to the total number of people exposed to a piece of content in a given period of time.

Audience Growth Rate: measures the speed that brand's social media following increases. Basically, it is a metric that describes how quickly you gain followers.(You can track your competitors' progress using this metric as well)
 – Measure your net new followers (on each platform) over time
 – Divide your net new followers by your total audience (on each platform) and multiply by 100 to get your audience growth rate percentage.

Interaction

Applause Rate: Is the number of Approval actions (such as likes, hearts, pins, etc) relative to the reach of the post. This metric is important because its an indicator of what your audience finds valuable about your content.
 – Add up the total approval actions a post received
 – Divide that number by your total followers and multiply by 100 to get your applause rate percentage.

Virality Rate: The % of people that shared the post versus the post reach.
 – Measure a post's impressions
 – Measure a post's shares

Average Engagement Rate: Is the number of Engagement actions (shares, comments, CTR, Landing Page views) relative to reach of the post. If you have a high engagement rate, the actual number of likes and comments don't matter. This is a very important metric to be keeping your eye on!
  – Add up a post's total likes, comments, and shares
  – Divide by your total number of followers and multiply by 100 to get your average engagement rate percentage.

Conversion

CTR (Click Through Rate): How often people click on a call–to–action link on a post. Your CTR is a metric specifically tied to an offer, outside link or landing page.
  – Measure the total clicks on a post's link.
  – Measure the total impressions on that post.
  – Divide the number of clicks by the number of impressions and multiply by 100 to get your CTR percentage.

Conversion Rate: Is the total number of conversions that came from your social media post, expressed as a percentage. For example, if you are posting about an event and 1,000 people see the post and 40 people click "I'm Going" and 10 people clicks "Maybe" then you have a conversion rate of 5%.

CPC (Cost–Per–Click): For a sponsored post or advertisement, a bidding system is used to determine how much you (the host of the post) (the post host) pays per click. You don't pay when the sponsored post or advertisement is shown, instead you pay every time it is clicked on.
  – Your CPC will help you determine if you are spending money efficiently on sponsored posts.
  – This metric can be found in your Ads Manager.

CPM (Cost Per 1,000 Impressions): (M = Latin for Mille, or 1,000). This is average cost you pay every time your sponsored post is seen 1,000 times.
  – This metric can be found in your Ads manager.

Landing Pages:

While it is important to have attractive, creative, and well-constructed social media, it is even more important that the content and links provided in social media posts take you to a place that will convert readers into taking further action, also known as a **Landing Page.** A Landing Page streamlines your customers' interaction with your brand and promotes long-term customer conversion.

Social Media Trust

Social Media is a massive sphere of "Word of Mouth". Personal endorsement is the consumer's most trusted source of information, and you will need trust in order to build your business.

Customer Testimonials
A Customer Testimonial is any customer review, comment, assessment, or endorsement relating to your brand. Customer Testimonials are the product of happy customers, and if they write a testimonial it means they are likely to share their good experience about your brand with other people via word of mouth. Also, having testimonials and reviews on your site or facebook page has been proven to increase conversion and consumer trust, even if its from people they don't know.

There are 3 essential platforms for customer testimonial – *Google Business, Yelp, Facebook.* You should then put these on your website in either the about section or on your landing page if you are pushing a product.

Run a social media campaign that encourages your best customers to create written, video, or online testimonials. I advise against offering to compensate them for their testimonial, because that would of course undermine your credibility as a brand.

Advertising vs Public Relations

Advertising: is creating paid announcements that bring a product (or service) to the attention of potential and current customers. This paid content placement is promoted through our social mediums by an advertiser to an audience.

Publicity & PR: Is a strategic communication process that mutually benefits the media author and the media reader. Public Relations is all about positioning your brand to be desirable for media outlets to talk about. PR can also be loosely defined as "Reputation Management".

5 Differences between Advertising and PR:

$$$

Advertising costs money to put your content into existing media. PR relies on positive media attention for your brand, which in turn creates a relationship between your brand and the media outlet. A legitimate media outlet will never ask for compensation for talking about your brand.

Control

In Advertising, you have complete creative control over your message, including where it will be seen and when it will be seen. In PR, you have much less control over your media coverage. Once you send your pitch to a journalist or editor, they take complete control over what is released. They can choose to change your story or do nothing at all. However, this can actually work to your benefit. If you send a pitch to multiple journalists, the story may be published in different ways. This means that your audience may see the story differently across different mediums which can reinforce the original message and purpose of the pitch.

Duration

The cost of advertising is duration based, meaning that you can run your ad for as long as you can continue paying for it. In PR, you are completely at the whims of the journalist. If you are receiving coverage from a popular digital publication, your story could be buried within hours of it being posted. If your story is run in print, then it will only be available in that edition of the print.

Credibility

Advertisements have much less credibility than earned coverage from Public Relations. When an audience sees an advertisement, they know that the placement has been bought by a company trying to sell them something. Public Relations provides newsworthy stories and information to journalists, who in-turn will write something about your brand in an unbiased manner. If the story is released, then you have also received a 3rd-party endorsement from the publication. This is why PR is considered to be such an important tool, because it has the power to shape public opinion about your brand. For example: Which would you trust more? An advertisement for my new album in Billboard Magazine? Or an album review from a journalist at Billboard Magazine?

Targeting

These days, digital Advertising lets you target your audience down to a science. Location, age, interests, hobbies, it is all broken down into bits of data that is then puzzled together to build a profile about who you are, what you do, and what you want. Don't let your romanticized perspective about data privacy fool you, Google and Facebook have been collecting data on you for a decade. Advertisers have been using this data to more efficiently target you with advertisements. While con- tent earned by Public relations will be confined to that media outlets audience.

As the old adage goes: *"Advertising is what you pay for, Publicity is what you Pray for"*

The 3 Audiences in Marketing

Cold Audience

A Cold Audience is a group of people that have never heard of your business. They are unfamiliar with your product and services and they are very difficult to pitch to. They are practically impossible to convert and yet, marketing to this audience is crucial.

You should target Cold Audiences to:
- Introduce your band or event
- Begin building a relationship with your customer
- Learn as much as possible about how they interact with your content
- Monitor their behavior on your website
- Target more relevant ads to convert them into a Warm Audience

Typically, you want to avoid directing a cold audience with a Landing Page right off the bat. Instead, consider offering a Cold Audience content that they value such as:
- Blog posts
- Videos
- Podcasts
- Cover Song Videos
- Music Lessons
- Music Gear Reviews

The most effective way to warm up a cold audience it to offer them a **lead magnet**, which is free resource that your audience perceive as valuable enough to submit their personal details in return for access.

You should also use **Conversion Tracking Pixels** to monitor your cold audiences behavior and then re-target them as they warm up to your brand. A Conversion Tracking Pixel keeps track of actions performed by your audience via Google Adwords or Facebook Ads manager. These actions include clicking on a button, signing up for a newsletter, completing a purchase, adding an item to a cart, visiting a product on you website, etc.

Once you have information about your customer (such as an email address or an associated facebook account, you need to start nurturing that relationship. There are 3 Important rules:
1. Offer value
2. Build trust
3. Confirm your authority

Warm Audience

A Warm Audience already knows who you are. They have connected with you on Social media, viewed your website, or joined a mailing list. You know that they are interested in the content, products and services you provide. But, so far, they have not indicated that they want to pay for a service

Your goal, therefore, is to drive this audience to content that delivers value to them, but also reinforces their interest in your product or services. Examples in the music world include:
- Hard Ticket Giveaways
- Q&A Interviews with band Members
- Reddit AMA's
- Lead Magnets, such as free music downloads
- Merchandise giveaways
- Music Videos
- Podcasts
- Song-Play-Through
- Exclusive content, such as a Pre-Release Album listening experience
- Any Offer that relates to your music or your performance.

If you have installed a "Conversion Tracking Pixel", you will be able to re-target your audience within incredibly specific parameters.

3 Examples of Warm Audience Re-targeting:

1. You could run a ticket giveaway to each show on a tour and only re-target warm audience members that live within a 25 mile radius of the show.

2. You could run a cover song music video at a warm audience that likes both your band and the original artist in attempt to convert them into buying a ticket to see your perform.

3. You could run an ad for an album pre-release online listening party via a webinar hosting site and target warm audience members that live in markets that your band wants to do better in.

Hot Audience

A Hot Audience are people that have paid money in exchange for your product or service. In the music industry, they are people that have paid to see you perform, bought merch, or purchased your music. These people are very familiar with your band and there is a good chance that they will continue to be so. You should have two goals in mind when marketing to your Hot Audience: Re-Engagement, and Up Sell. You should be trying to get this audience to buy from you again or to re-engage with customers who haven't bought from you in a long time.

Your don't need to convince them of your value anymore, but rather remind them of your products in hopes that they buy again. Drive your Hot Audience to:
– Sales Pages
– Landing Pages
– Offer pages
– Product Pages

Webpages to drive a Hot Audience:
– New Album Landing Page
– Hard Ticket Show Event Page
– New Merchandise Offer Page
– Tour Announcement

Things to Remember about Social Marketing:

– Selling a product is a 3-step process

– Different people have different needs

– Different people have different knowledge about your brand

– Build Relationships = More willing consumers

– Cold Audience conversion is practically impossible

– Your Music is your marketing, not your product

– Pay attention to what platform your audience is on and market on those platforms

– Give more value than you take

– Every post is an "ask" for consumer attention

– When you give with expectation in return – you lose

Facebook Advertising

Facebook Advertising is currently the best way to reach new audiences. Facebook's detailed targeting lets you narrow down your marketed audience to a science. The majority of Fortune 500 Companies are not running ads on Facebook, meaning the cost of running these advertisements in early 2019 is under-priced.

Facebook Advertising not only lets you target new audiences, but it can re-target your existing fan-base as well, something called a *Custom Audience*. You can upload your database of email lists into facebook and show ads to everyone on that list with an associated facebook account. You can also import data and run ads at people that have been to your website via a Facebook Pixel. This is a line of code on your website that grabs a cookie of information about the visitor, allowing you to run ads at that person for up to 90 days after they visit your website.

Facebook algorithms highly restrict organic post reach and running ads has become the new normal. Because of this, you may not want to run ads with the intent of having people like your facebook page, but instead use your ads to promote some other product – such as promoting a landing page, facebook event page, album release awareness, email sign-up, or video views.

Steps for Creating and Running a Facebook Ad Campaign

Step 1: Determine your Intent.
What is the purpose of your Ad? Is it to spread awareness about your album or tour? And most importantly, is it measurable? The more detailed you make your intent, the better you be able to measure its success. Facebook ads will let you drive traffic to your website, landing page or event page, build brand awareness, video views, email sign-ups, and much more.

2. Determine your Budget.
Facebook ads work on Auction, a sort of bidding system where ads compete with other for screen time. The cost of running each ad is determined by targeting parameters and competition. If an audience is more expensive to run ads at because more advertisers are competing

against each other and raising the **bid** (ad price). Facebook sells screen placement of an ad to whomever is willing to pay the highest price.

An expensive target audience is usually the result of that audience being willing or more able to purchase a product. Which is why it is cheaper to advertise to 13–18 year old men than 35–50 year old women. Facebook will let you run ads on a daily budget or a lifetime budget, and you can cancel your ad at any time. If you want to test the waters to see how an ad performs, you can set it up to run a 2$ daily budget. If it runs well, you can increase that budget to whatever you like.

3. Determine your Target Audience.
 – Who do you want to see your ad and why?
 – Are you advertising efficiently? (Meaning that only the people you want to see your ad are seeing your ad)

Facebook allows you to target incredibly niche areas, which means you don't have to waste money showing your ad to people who don't care. Below is a list of targeting parameters that you should explore:
 – People who already like your Facebook page
 – Friends of people who like your Facebook page
 – People who are interested in bands similar to yours
 – People who live in your city (if you're trying to build a local fan-base)
 – People who live in cities where you plan on touring
 – People who have engaged with your Facebook videos
 – People who have visited your website (you'll need to install a Facebook pixel to do this)
 – People who have subscribed to your email list
 – Lookalike audiences of any custom audiences you've created

4. Create Your Ad
Head on over to Facebook Ads Manager and make a business account. You will need to connect a credit card and a facebook page. There are 5 different types of formats for Advertisements on Facebook:
 – Photo
 – Video
 – Carousel
 – Slide-show
 – Messenger

Additionally, you ad can contain a "call to action" button such as a "Learn More", "Visit Site", or "Sign-Up". When creating a new ad in Facebook Ad Manger you will be guided step by step through the advertisement details:
- *Objective* (The purpose or intent of the ad)
- *Audience* (To whom the ad will be shown)
- *Budget* (How much you are willing to spend to show ad)
- *Schedule* (When the ad will be shown)
- *Placement* (where the ad will be shown)

You can also "Boost" an existing post that is performing well organically. Doing this will limit some of your creative and targeting options, so I would recommend just making an ad with the high performing content.

5. Review you Ad analytics
While your advertisement is running, you should keep an eye on its performance and make updates as needed. Facebook Ads Manager will give you detailed metrics in real time about the performance and efficiency of your advertisement.

You should alway A+B your advertisements, which is a split test that tests two variables against each other. In this, you can prepare two different subject lines, pictures, or copywrite and test the ads against each other to see which one performs better.

Facebook Advertising Metrics:

CPM: Cost per 1,000 Impressions

CPE: Cost Per Engagement

CPLV: Cost Per Landing Page View

Reach: Unique Views

Frequency: Average number of times the advertisement is shown to the same person

Engagement: The number of post clicks, likes, shares, comments, or actions on your post

Amount Spent: how much you've spent running your ads so far. This is set by you in the Budget section of your ad sets.

CTR: Click Through Rate: the percent of people who saw your ad and clicked over to your opt-in page. Calculated by taking the number of Link Clicks and dividing it by Impressions.

Link Clicks: the number of people who clicked on your ad and were directed to your opt-in page. This is a good metric to use to estimate the number of people who visited your opt-in page (unless you're sending people to the same opt-in page from all different sources, which I don't recommend).

CPC (Cost Per Click): the average cost of each click from your ad over to your website. Calculated by taking the Amount Spent divided by the number of Link Clicks.

Cost per Lead: how much each sign-up has cost you so far. Calculated by taking the Amount Spent and dividing it by the number of Leads.

Example of a Facebook Advertisement Campaign

Promoting a Music Video

Advertisement: Cover song/Video of an original song
Intent: Video Views
Budget: 100$ over 5 days (20$ a day)

Target Audience:
- Audiences that "Like" Your Band
- Audiences that "Like" artists that are similar to yours (RIYL)
- Audiences Aged 13–40, Male and Female
- Audiences living in **Markets that you want to sell more tickets**
- Custom Audience made of people that have signed up for your email list database or have visited your website in the last 90 days

Placement:
- Facebook News Feed (Desktop),
- Facebook News Feed (Mobile),
- Instagram News Feed

Target Analytics:
- *CPE* = $0.05
- *CPM* = $0.15
- *Impressions*: 667,000
- *Frequency* = 1 – 7
- *Reach* = # of Impressions / Frequency
- *Engagement*: 2,000 likes, comments, shares, or post interactions

Additional Benefits:
- Organic reach and engagement from Shares. (Once a video is shared from an ad, it doesn't appear as an ad in other people's news feed meaning you start receiving organic engagement.)
- Plenty of people to re-target with an event page or tour poster later
- The general hype around your brand increases

Snapchat Advertising

What is a Snapchat advertisement?

Snapchat ads are 3–10 second vertical videos that appear in between friend stories and curated content, such as Snapchat stories and publishers stories. Snapchat users can swipe up at any time during the video for more information – either to view a longer video (up to 10 minutes), read an article, install an app, or visit a website.

Why use Snapchat for advertising? **

- 188 Million users on the app daily
- Each user spends an average of 30 minutes on the app per day
- Each use opens the app an average of 18 times per day
- Of those users, 35% cannot be reached on Facebook, 46% cannot be reached on Instagram, and 81% cannot be reached on Twitter.
- Advertisers can target Snapchat users based on their demographics and online interests and behaviors.
- Advertisers can use their own data to reach customers on Snapchat
- Snapchat Ads are played Full Screen, and can receive two times as much visual attention as other social media ads
- Snapchat Ads are played with volume 60% of the time (compared to only 15% for facebook ads)
- Snapchat Ads "swipe-up" feature is **5 times higher** than the average click through rate of other social media ads.

Ages of Snapchat Users

- 13–17 (22%)
- 18–24 (36%)
- 25–34 (27%)
- 35+ (15%)

How to make Snapchat ads

Snapchat Ads Manager is very similar to Facebook Ads Manager. SAM (Snapchat Ads Manager) uses the same 3–step structure for creating ads as Facebook: *Campaign*, *Ad Sets*, and *Ads*.

** *Statistics from Media Science*

Step 1: Determine your Objective
– *"Drive Traffic to my website"*
– *"Grow Awareness"*
– *"Drive Installs of my App"*
– *"Drive Video Views"*

After you choose your Snapchat ad's objective, give it a name.

Keep in mind that Snapchat does not automatically save your progress in Ad creation, so you won't be able to recover your work if you do not complete the ad in one sitting.

Step 2: Determine your Audience
You can narrow your target audience into 5 different categories:

Geography
– Country, State, City, X Mile Radius around a location

Demographics
– Age, gender, language, income, parental status, and more

Audiences
– What they like, what they've bought, where they've been, what they've watched
– You can also upload your own audience data and directly target your customers, as well as create Lookalike Audiences.

Placements
– Snapchat Stories or Publishers content
– Friends Stories
– Both

Device
– Type of Phone and Operating System

Snapchat will not let you target an audience of less than 1,000 people.

Step 3: Determine your Budget

Snapchat ads work on Auction, a sort of bidding system. When determining your budget, Snapchat will ask you to put down your desired bid amount. Snapchat will then show your advertisement to your audience when your ad wins the bid. The cost of running each ad is determined by your targeting parameters and amount of competition.

Certain audiences are more expensive to run ads against because more advertisers are competing against each other, thus raising the bid. An expensive target audience is the result of that audience being more willing to purchase a product.

Step 4: Create Your Ad

Snapchat has 4 Ad Formats:

Top Snap Only
3 – 10 second video ad with no Call To Action or "Swipe Up"*Web View*
Drive traffic to your website

App Install
Drive traffic to an app page in Google Play or Apple App Store

Long-Form Video
10 second trailer that leads to a long form video, up to 10 minutes long.

From here, you will need to upload a few details about your ad:

Brand Name
 – Maximum 25 characters

Headline
 – Maximum 34 characters

Call to Action
 – What do you want the consumer to do?

Media File
 – Build from scratch, upload your own, or use a pre–designed template
 – *"The trick is to film videos on iPhones using the front facing camera with the talent front and center — and with no branding until three to five seconds in" according to Liam Copeland. "The more organic the ad feels and the later the branding appears, the more likely a user is to swipe up to view long-form content or web content," he said.*

Upload your attachment/action
 – Website, long form video, or app page.

Step 5: Monitor the Ad
Monitor the performance, edit the schedule, edit the budget, and prepare a report of the results. You can download your ad results in a CSV file. Here are the details of your campaign and ad set that you can edit once your ad is launched:

Campaign:
 – Campaign name
 – Daily budget (This has to be larger than 70 percent of the sum of daily budgets of all ad sets within the campaign.)
 – Schedule
 – Status

Ad set:
 – Ad set name
 – Schedule
 – Daily budget
 – Bid amount

Snapchat Advertising Metrics

Impressions

Total Impressions: The total number of times a Snapchatter saw your Brand as either the Story Tile or the individual Snap.

Paid Impressions: The total number of times a Snapchatter saw the Story Tile on the stories page. Counted when the tile is 50% on screen for at least 1 second.

Position Impressions: The total number of times a Snapchatter saw the individual Snap Ads inside the story. Counted after a Snapchatter clicks in the story tile and the Snap fully renders on the screen.

Total ecPM: Effective cost per thousand total impressions, which includes paid and Story impressions.

Reach

Total Reach: The total number of Snapchatters who viewed your Brand as either the Story Tile or the individual Snaps.

Paid Reach: The total number of Snapchatters who viewed your Brand as the Story Tile.

Story / Earned Reach: The total number of Snapchatters who viewed an individual Snap within your Story Ad.

Engagement

Story Opens: The total amount of times Snapchatters tapped on the tile.

Story Open Rate: The rate at which Snapchatters tapped on the tile.

Swipe Ups: The total number of times a Snapchatter has swiped up on attachments within your Story Ad (aggregated across all attachments).

Swipe Up Rate: The rate at which Snapchatters swiped up on swipeable top Snaps to reveal the attachment below (averaged across all attachments).

Average Attachment Screen Time: The average number of seconds spent viewing your attachment across all impressions (averaged across all attachments).

Completed Story Views: The total number of times a Snapchatter views through to the end of your Story Ad.

Snapchat Geofilter Advertising

What is a Geofilter?

A Geofilter is a location based Snapchat filter. With On–Demand geofilters, anyone can pay to create their own geofilter in a specific area for a set amount of time. Geofilters have a minimum size of 5,000, a minimum duration of 30 minutes, and pricing begins at 5$ a day per 20,000 square feet.

Snapchat geofilters offer huge competitive advantage for traveling bands and businesses because not a lot of bands, especially up and coming ones, are using geofilters. Spapchat offers Personal (does not include any branding, logos, business names or trademarks) and Branded (for Business) geofilters. Filters cannot contain any photographs of people, URL's, phone numbers and emails. Snapchat Geofilters have a maximum size of 5 Million square feet, and a maximum of 30 days.

How to Create a Geofilter

Step 1: Design your filter
 – 1080 x 1920 dimensions
 – Transparent background .PNG format
 – Under 300kb in size
 – Text can cover only 25% of the screen

Step 2: Upload your Filter
 – Head over to Snapchat.com/on–demand and click "Create Now". You will need to sign in to your existing Snapchat account. Then it's as simple as uploading your file.

Step 3: Set the Date, Time, and Location
 – Make sure you are only paying for your filter when and where the event is actively happening.

Step 4: Launch your Filter

Step 5: Review your Analytics
 – Review your $$ spend and compare your actual costs vs expected costs of running the ad

TOURING

Booking a Tour
Promoting a Tour
Going On Tour
Advancing the Show
Music Industry Roles, Rates, and Responsibilities
The Business Manager

Booking A Tour

Know your Deals

Door Deal: % of the money made at the door via Ticket Sales.

Guarantee: Flat Fee that is Guaranteed to the artist no matter the venue income or expenses related to the show.

Vs Deal: Flat Fee VS Door Deal, whichever one is higher in favor of the artist.

Split Point: Which is a deal where by the artist has a guarantee, but also has the opportunity to make more money based on venue expenses and ticket revenue. *How to calculate:*
(Box Office) – (Tax) – (Expenses) – (Artist Guarantee) = (The Split Point)

Here's an example. You have a guarantee of 500$. The Box Office revenue is 1,000$. The venue expenses are 250$. The tax is 50$.

$1000 – $50 – $250 – $500 = 200$

That **200$** is the *Split Point.*

When you reach the Split Point, that is called *"Going into Points"*. Any overage past the Split point is then split per a previously negotiated Percentage. So in this scenario, if you have an 80% Split point deal, you will be walking home with 160$ from the points plus your guarantee of 500 for a total of 660$

Prepare a Stage Plot

A Stage Plot is a list of Inputs, Outputs, and Stage directions for the venue production staff. Your stage plot should include:
 – Instruments & Amp Type
 – Power Needed
 – Mics needed
 – A complete and accurate I/O (Input / Output list)
 – Preference on Stage Position (diagram)

Consider the Underplay

It is easy to get caught up in the numbers game. And that's because the most important component of social marketing is non-quantifiable. You can't turn it into numbers. You can't measure it, you can only measure the results. That thing, is HYPE. An **underplay** is a show that is guaranteed to sell-out because the venue capacity is so much smaller than the expected attendance.

Search for Local Support

It is unlikely that your band will be booked as out-of-town support for a local Headliner. Much more likely, is that you will be an out-of-town headliner with local support. Paying attention to which local band is going to support your headlining bill is a hidden gem that many club level bands completely ignore. You can essentially co-opt the entire fan-base of a well picked local support act. This is not only good strategy for long-term market growth, but is also a healthy tit-for-tat in the concert industry. You provide an event just out of reach of the local act to do by themselves, and in turn they offer you the chance to impress their audience.

If you are a small local band looking to be booked onto a larger show this way, you need to starve your home market and build as much hype as you can. I know that this sounds paradoxical, but its simple *Supply and Demand*. The goal here is to create as much demand as possible content and press while limiting the opportunity for people to pay to see you play at a venue. Doing this correctly will give you huge leverage over other bands that the Promoter may be considering.

If you are a Touring band, do some research into the scene as to what bands have hype in that city and reach out to them directly. Be prepared to sacrifice some of the financial security of the show in exchange for them pulling a large crowd. Offer to split a % of the back end or even a % of the door.

Radius Clauses

A *radius clause* is a time frame or geographic restriction that prevents an artist from playing a competing show. Standard radius Clause is 60 Days and 60 Miles and can be found in the performance Contract. It gives the promoter a form of territorial exclusivity over the performance. If get caught breaking a radius clause, that is legal justification for the promoter to remove you from the show. Radius Clauses are almost always found in contracts for soft-ticket events. Make sure your manager is reviewing the performance contracts just in case you over-looked a radius clause.

** *Tandem: If you accidentally break a radius clause, please let the affected parties know immediately and try to make amends. We are all human. But if you shrug it off.... Get ready for some trash-talk.*

Tour Budgeting

Before you leave for tour, the TM should make a list of expected incomes and expenses while on the road. Don't forget to include a safety net for things like the van breaking down or a medical emergency. When making a tour budget, remember that fewer expenses is better than greater income. Download Gas apps for finding cheap gas, sleep on cots in stranger's houses. Eat as much free food as you can find, and bring a cooler with you for storing leftovers and snacks. If you are a coffee drinker, I recommend taking caffeine pills instead. *Try and save money everywhere you can.*

Attracting a Booking Agent

A Booking agent only cares about 2 things: How many tickets do you sell and where do you sell them.

Tertiary Markets: the smallest of the three classification of market size. This is a small city or town, somewhere with a population of less than 50,000 people. Doing well in these markets can often be attributed to a limited nightlife and music scene. Or its the hometown of one of your band members, and you pack the club out with your homies. These markets do not have theaters, but small clubs or large bars.

Secondary Markets: The middle classification of market size. The majority of your touring will be spent in Secondary markets. These are small – large cities with populations between 50k and 1 million. These markets have large theaters, several clubs, developed arts communities, and an active nightlife.

Primary Markets: These are really big cities: (In the US) LA, Atlanta, Dallas, New York City, Toronto, Seattle, Nashville, Boston & Chicago. Success in Primary markets is the most valuable to a booking agent.

In the US, you are ready to approach serious booking agents about representation once you have established ten 100 person markets. As your band grows, you will open up opportunities to work with better and better agents that can get you better and better shows. The next tier will be ten 300 person markets, then, and then from there ten 1,000 person markets, and then 5,000 person markets and so on.

The Booking Agent Catch 22

How do you build markets if you don't have a booking agent?
How do you get a booking agent if you haven't built any markets?

The answer: you just have to do it yourself for a while.

Your tickets sales numbers are the most important thing to pitch to booking agencies. Sure, your album was produced by a Grammy winning producer and your publicist landed you an interview on KEXP and your grandmother loves you and thinks your band is great but a booking agent only cares about 2 Things:

(1) How many tickets

(2) In which markets

Promoting A Tour

Make a Promo Page

A Promo Page is an invisible page on your website that acts as a digital tool for promoters to access necessary information about your band.

Your promo Page should have:
 - Contact information for the band's Management, Booking Agency, and Publicist
 - Online Resources section with hyper-links to the bands Social Media and website
 - One paragraph Bio / Description about the Band.
 - At Least 3 Press Photos with Photo Credit
 - Tour Admat / Poster (hi-res)
 - Video files available for Direct Download (hi-res)
 - Promo video for the Tour / Show (2 versions: 60 second for IG and a full-length for FB)
 - Hyper-links and Embed code for Latest music via 2 streaming platforms (Bandcamp and Spotify)

In-Studio Performances and Ticket Giveaways

Use these as promo while on tour 2 or 3 weeks. Before your performance, look up the contact information for college radio stations, non-commercial radio stations, and local newspapers. For Radio Stations, you want to contact the MD, or Music Director. And for newspapers, you want to contact the arts/humanities/culture editor or assistant editor if they have one. Send them a quick email explaining who you are, where and when you are playing, and ask if they would be willing to do a ticket giveaway. Usually the band is given a guest list when you can put ticket giveaway winners, so you don't necessarily have to ask permission for this as long as you stay organized.

It is mutually beneficial for these places to piece together a blurb about your show because (1) It is an opportunity for them to interact with the community and (2) talking about your show can be just the piece of content that they needed that week.

If the radio station or newspaper is particularly interested, you could ask for an in-studio performance or interview which can be great for your show! Just make sure that the logistics line up appropriately before committing to one.

Instagram and Snapchat Takeover Stories

The *"Story Takeover"* is an excellent way to build awareness about a show and reach a broader audience. A Story Takeover is exactly what it sound like! You, as the band, post on the venue's story to promote your show. You will need to get in contact with whoever is running the social media for your event – whether it's the venue or the promoter.

You should prepare a script and record yourself in advance of the tour, less than 15 seconds in vertical format. Or, you can free-style it the day of. Regardless, you will want to quickly introduce yourselves and announce the show as quickly as possible. Adding a humor element is a good idea – funny costumes, or an interesting/compromising situation (such as in the bathroom of a gas station).

Email videos out to the venue as a download link, not an attachment. Make sure your videos are in .mp4 format. Also, I should note that if you are not the headlining act on the show, you will need to get permission from the headliner's PR team, and in some cases you won't be able to do this at all.

Street Team

The Marketing term for a group of people that "hit the streets" to promote an event or a product. The Street Team model was developed by Urban Record Labels, who found it to be a cost efficient medium of communication to their target audience, many of whom were non-accessible via the traditional marketing outlets of Print, Radio, and Television. It was and still is a working form of marketing for brands & artists that creates hype through credible peer-to-peer interactions and word-of-mouth marketing.

Most venues and promoters already have an established Street Team that handles their physical promo.

But if you are really trying to get ahead of the game, you can create your own. Of course, you will have to incentivize them somehow!

Google forms can collect emails and information about your street team members and then you should send them the Posters for the show, handbills, digital content, etc, with very specific instructions on where and how to post. Make sure that you ask for Proof that they completed their task. Street team coordination is deceptively time consuming and shouldn't be taken lightly.

Venue Contacts

Once you've booked the show, you, the agent, the venue, and the promoter are all pretty much on the same side. So no matter what, if you have any questions or need help promoting your show, ask the venues to help. Because if you have a successful show, then they have a successful show.

Established venues will often send you a list of local promotion contacts, such as radio and print promotion, digital magazines, blogs, and routes for your street team to put their posters. And even though this is normally highly guarded information, they will share it with you because the venue, the agent, and the promoter need you to do well way more than you think.

PR Stunts

All press is good press. If you have a crazy idea that might just work, I say go for it! Here are some of my favorite examples of PR stunts that absolutely worked in favor of the artist despite the publics reaction.

Alice Cooper, Piccadilly Square

Alice Cooper was booked to play the Wembley Arena in London which is a 10,000 person room, and they had only sold 50 tickets. Alice Cooper's Manager, Shep Gordon (a huge figure in Music Industry PR) came up with a plan. They superimposed a picture of Alice Cooper naked except for a snake covering his nether regions onto the side of a billboard truck with the name, date and time of the show.

They hired a driver and instructed him to drive the billboard truck into Piccadilly square, the busiest intersection in London, and sincerely pretend that the billboard truck had broken down. Shep Gordon also anonymously hit up the press with information that something that was going to go down, to make sure that the Press was in position to get high-quality photos of the show details.

That afternoon, London came to a standstill and Alice Cooper became the most hated man in the country. Every news station in the UK jumped onto the bandwagon to talk about Cooper's negligence and irresponsibility. The next day all 10,000 tickets were sold. By the end of the week, Alice Cooper's single "School's Out" was #1 on the global Billboard Chart.

Even crazier is that this stunt reportedly only cost $5,000 to pull off and the largest expense was paying the driver to get arrested.

Banksy

On October 16th, 2018 Banksy shredded his own painting, "Girl with Balloon", the moment it sold at auction for 1.3 million dollars. Maybe he was trying to inspire change in the art community. Maybe the man is a "provocateur, unafraid to critique the exorbitant high-prices of the art market". Or, because the shredded work was actually appraised at a higher value post-shredding than what it sold for, maybe it was an attempt at increasing his own self-worth. So much so, that some people argue the auction-house, Sotheby's, was even in on it.

Regardless, this was a monster of a PR stunt and it vaulted him back into the public eye and twitter-sphere. Make of this what you will, but know that the image of the shredded painting and gasps from the crowd has been shared hundreds of thousands of times on social media accounts around the world.

Hip-Hop

I cannot verify this PR stunt. I've searched and searched for verification and I have not found any. It may not have happened, but regardless this is a really good stunt. It takes some social media leverage and a younger, bolder audience to pull off.

So the idea is, a rapper is trying to promote his new album. And so immediately after the release, he makes a call to his Instagram followers to sneak into their school offices where the intercom is and play one of his songs over the intercom to the entire school. And if they can prove that they did it, he would feature them on his channel.

This is so smart because It's a community building moment for him and his fans, it's great exposure for the new album, and it's basically has zero cost or risk for the artist. And so, all these kids around the country are getting suspended from school for playing his album over the intercom and he delivered on his promise to feature them. And now he's got this great relationship with his community because he followed through for his fans plus he garnered exposure from the stunt.

Going On Tour

Designate a Tour Manager

The Tour Manager, or TM, is the director of all of the artist's business and professional activity. Tour Manager responsibilities include:
- Answering the phone
- Resolving crisis on the road
- Reading Contracts
- Recording Expenses
- Logging Mileage
- Showing Up On-Time
- Getting the money

Tour Admat / Poster

Industry standard size for a tour poster is 11 inches by 17 inches. Your tour poster should have all of your dates with your name/logo displayed prominently. Here's the catch, venues don't care about other shows on your tour poster, which is why the artist is also expected to prepare advertising materials to the venue.

Ad Mat is an abbreviation of Advertising Material and is usually a derivation of your tour poster. Except, instead of all of your tour dates listed, the poster has empty space for the venue to write in their own information. Venues prefer to write all of this in themselves, and that's a good thing because this way you only have to prepare 1 Ad Mat to send to each venue.

Cases for your Gear

I know that road cases are expensive, but the cost of the case is usually less than the cost to repair. The road is a vulnerable and dangerous place for your gear. There are a lot of things that can go wrong and protecting your equipment is paramount! Car accidents, trailer problems, sketchy load-in, sketchy neighborhoods, Gear bouncing around and crashing into each other on bumpy roads.

Many times you will have to leave your instruments, pedals, and accessories in less than ideal places, like mop closets, dark hallways, or even stacked against a venue wall for extended periods of time.

If you are involved in a fast changeover on stage, you might not even be handling your own instrument. Without your gear you have no livelihood. I recommend checking your local pawn shops, who are known for having an excess of musical cases. Also check Ebay for custom sized cases.

Musicians Insurance

Some homeowner, renters, or automobile insurance policies cover musical items that are taken out of the house, but this is generally not the case. Musicians Insurance covers your instruments, recording gear, sound and light equipment, computer hardware, and various audio accessories.

Additionally, standard insurance providers might not recognize the actual value of your gear. And in the event of a large claim, like a break-in, car accident, or venue fire, you will hit a per-category limit on your insurance and you might receive much less than what the gear is worth. You can take out a basic policy for up to $12,000 worth of gear for a little over 10$ a month.

I'm not going to suggest any particular insurance company, but regardless of who you choose you will need to make an itemized list of all your gear. Definitely do some research and get some insurance. Hopefully you won't need it but if you do, you will be glad you have it.

An Effective Merch Table

Your Merch table should function like an in-person marketing funnel. When someone walks up to your merch table, that is a pivotal engagement between you and a potential customer! And so you need to make it as easy as possible for your fans to give you their information, make a purchase, or generally connect with your brand.

A couple tips about the Merch Table:

– Collect information for whichever platform you are most comfortable with. Snapchat, Instagram, Facebook, Email marketing. Whatever you choose, make sure you are using their information to your advantage. Invest in some art or decorations for your merch table, such as a fancy price sign, tablecloth, suitcase, etc. You want your merch table to be so beautiful that people take pictures and put it on Pinterest!

– Quick transactions!
Invest in a POS, which stands for Point Of Sale, system that can quickly process debit card transactions and keep track of inventory.

– Order at least twice as many mediums and larges as you order smalls, XL's, and 2XL's. The secret to selling a shit-load of merch is to understand that the merch table is where consumers buy accessories to the experience. Your consumer often doesn't really want or need a shirt or as a lighter, or a pair of sunglasses, the consumer wants to take home a piece of the band with them, and so they decide which format of that experience they like the most and then they buy it.

Your job as the band is to project the experience of your music into material items that can be manufactured and sold at a 400% margin. You get bonus points if you have things on your merch table that folks actually need, such as ponchos at a rainy outdoor show.

Take care of your teeth.

Health Insurance is unlikely in the cards for you, so make sure you are at least taking care of your teeth. Wrap your toothbrush in a paper towel in a ziploc bag so it stays clean on the road. Dental Hygiene is no joke. Not only is it a form of preventative healthcare but brushing your teeth in the morning and before you go to bed is a routine.

Consistency can be hard to find to find on the road. So the act of brushing your teeth is actually a form of commitment to the longevity of your career as a professional musician. If you can't handle brushing your teeth on the road, then you are not going to make it very far in this crazy industry.

2 More Tips:

– Every time your van stops, get out of the van and stretch. Remaining in stasis (not moving) can be really damaging on your body and mental health. Keeping your blood moving while on a long drive to your next show is actually incredibly important. Don't be a lazy bum and nap the whole ride. Hop out and do some jumping jacks or do some stretches. 10 years from now, you will thank yourself for it.

– Keep all of your receipts and log your mileage for tax purposes. When you write off your taxes (in the US), you actually get more money back if you log mileage instead of gas charges, so keep a log of mileage at the beginning and end of your tours. You will also need to know mileage to calculate the depreciation of your van at the end of the year (another tax write-off).

Advancing The Show

Confirming in advance the details surrounding your show with the venue or promoter.

Advancing the Show is the process of confirming the details of your performance with the venue or the promoter in advance of the show (1–3 days). Once you have confirmed your show, the booking agent will send and sign a performance contract with all of the necessary show details.

At this point, you should collect the name, email, and phone number for your **point of contact** for the show. The point of contact is the Venue Manager, Production Manager, Promoter, Talent Buyer, or any person that can confirm details about the show on behalf of the venue.

What to ask the Promoter when Advancing the Show:
– What kind of physical promo is being prepared for the show?
     Poster's, Flyers, Handbills, etc
– Who is responsible for creating physical Promo such as posters?
– The Artist or The Promoter
– When do tickets go on sale?
– Is there a ticket Pre-Sale?
– Has the local media been notified of the show?
– Will the venue/promoter share their directory of local publicity outlets?
     Radio Stations
     Blogs
     Magazines
     Newspapers

Performance Contract

Your Performance Contract outlines the details, finances and deal structure of your performance. Attached to the Performance Contract are additional specifics on behalf of the artist for the venue that "ride" on top of the contract. These are called **riders**, and your performance contract will include a Hospitality Rider and Technical Rider.

Performance Contract Details
- Name and Address of Venue
- Directions to the venue
- Parking for Load In / During the Show
- Load In Time
- Sound Check Time
- Doors Opening Time
- Show Time
- Set Length
- Is there a **Hall Fee**? (A % of the Merch sales paid to the venue)

Hospitality Rider
- Accommodations for special hospitality needs
- Name and Address of where you are staying
- Who is paying for it?
- Food provided to the artist
- Who is paying for it?
- Is there a **Runner**? (A person or persons hired to act as personal shopper or driver for the band and crew)
- Security personnel
- Access to private bathrooms, shower, or dressing room
- # Of complimentary tickets ("comps") or guest list

Technical Rider
- Stage Plot
- Input List
- Sound System Specifics
- Lighting package
- Backline availability
- Crew available on site for assisting the crew
- Accommodations for special technical needs

Music Industry Roles, Rates, & Responsibilities

Booking Agent:

- Arranges Concerts
- Is paid 10% of the Artist Performance Fee
- Typically Exclusive
- Routes tour
- Negotiates contracts with the promoter or talent buyer
- Sets ticket price

$$$ – How Much They're Paid

- 10% of the Artist Performance Fee
- Tour Manager sends the commission to the Agent
- The TM collects money only for shows the Agents has booked

Promoter/Talent Buyer

- "Buys the Talent"
- Takes the Risk
- Hires Artist to play at venues
- The Promoter deals directly with the Booking Agents

$$$ – How Much They're Paid

- A negotiated % of the Show Net Profit
- If the show is not profitable, the Promoter loses money

Attorney

- Reviews and negotiates all contracts
- Assists booking agent on performance contracts
- Assists manager on recording contracts
- Assists band on manager Contracts

$$$ – How Much They're Paid

- Hourly, typically on retainer

This means that the client (artist) will pay the attorney a lump sum of money upfront, say 10 hours worth, to keep the attorney available to work on your contracts if need be.

The attorney will be paid from the "retainer" sum until they finish their work or go over the 10 hour limit. They will not continue their work until the overage is paid. An excess of retainer money can be refundable or non-refundable, depending on your lawyer. If your attorney wants to charge you a retainer for an excessive number of hours and it is non-refundable, go find a different lawyer.
  - OR 5% of the artists gross income

Publicist
  - Arranges Press coverage
        Album reviews, concert reviews, features, video premieres, & in-person appearances
  - Arranges radio and magazine interviews
  - Not necessarily exclusive, but coordinated
  - Hired for terms of 3-6 months

$$$ - How Much They're Paid
  - Monthly fee over the course of the publicity campaign

Manager
  - Leader of the bands business activity
  - Decision maker in all aspects of the band's career (typically exclusive)
  - *"Builds bridges and puts out fires"*
  - 2 types of managers:
        Contract
        Handshake
  - Develops Tour in conjunction with Booking Agent (*Except in CA & NY*)
  - May select support acts
  - Negotiates merchandise price, items
  - Hires/Fires Tour crew members
  - Negotiates general terms of a record deal
  - Select the producer, session musicians, and studio for a record
  - Affected by the "Sunset Clause"
        Sunset Clause: The Manager will continue receiving payment for past work at a rate and for a duration as specified by this clause. For example: *10 % at 6 months, 5 % at 12 months, 2.5% at 18 months, 0% at 24 Months*

$$$ – How Much They're Paid
 – 15–20% of the artist's Gross Income
 – Advances are typically not–commissioned

FOH Engineer

The Front of House Engineer mixing audio for the audience. They work in the center of the crowd in a large venue and are paid by the promoter or brought on by the band.

Monitor Engineer

The Monitor Engineer mixes audio for the members of the band on stage and is usually located on or near the stage. They are paid by the promoter or brought on by the band.

Lighting Designer

A lighting Designer, or LD, works to create the lighting, atmosphere, art installation, and visual effects of a show. The LD operates a light board during the show which can be controlled either by hand or by software. They are paid by the promoter or brought on by the band.

The Business Manager

Long-term financial stability is the crux of every artist in the world:
What can we afford to save and reinvest in ourselves?
What can we afford to go on tour?
What can we afford to put out a new record?
What wan we afford to pay ourselves every month?
Can we turn our passion into a business?

A **Business Manager** can answer these questions for you, and is an eventual necessity in your career. Your business manager will:
- Handle all of the Money
- Pay Taxes
- Build Tour Budget
- Be responsible for accounting all income and expenses
- Issue paychecks for crew, band members
- Double check the numbers
- Oversee the recording budget
- Pay all bills related to production
- Collect all royalties
- Say NO to ideas if they are over budget

$$$ - How Much They're Paid
- 5% of artist's Gross Income OR Hourly on retainer
- Collects commission only while working

Paying Taxes

If you are going to make money as an artist and be a business, you have to pay your taxes. This is the most common responsibility of a business manager, and the IRS always gets their money. But I have good news! You are not going to believe what you can write off on your taxes and how much money you can save.

As long as you make at least $500 of self-employed income as a working musician or touring artist, you can write off:

- All Transportation by Bus, Plane, Train, or Car

- Local transportation by Public Transit, Taxis, Ridesharing such as Lyft, and Car Rentals
- Most Lodging
- Shipping and Baggage fees
- Laundry and Dry Cleaning
- Remote Internet Access & Web hosting
- Some professional Memberships related to the Music Industry
- Trade publication subscriptions
- Demo Recordings
- Agent or Manager Fees and Commissions
- Professional education that maintains or improves your skill
- Promotional Tickets for people that may hire you in the future
- Sub musicians, assistants, side musicians, accompanists, and temps
- Rehearsal and Studio rental Instrument and Equipment rental
- Concert attire
- Instruments and Equipment purchased
- Professional Research, such as sheet music, recordings, concert tickets, and even music festivals
- Business Miles
- Parking and Tolls
- Depreciation on the Band vehicle

To qualify as a business and write off these expenses, you must prove to the IRS that your career as a musician is in attempt to supplement earning a living, even if you are just doing it as an enthusiast or as a hobby, hence the $500 minimum income requirement. Your expenses must also be both ordinary and necessary as decided by the IRS, so document anything you want to write off via Bank Statements or photos of receipts.

I am not a tax professional and I do not claim to be. I can tell you, that if you are making money as a band and you want to continue to do so, you must pay your taxes.

You, or rather your business manager, needs to talk to a Certified Public Accountant, preferably one that has experience with traveling businesses or the entertainment industry.

Bonus Points: *Your business manager is also a CPA*

THE ALBUM RELEASE

A (brief) History of the Industry
Album Pre–Order
Record Labels
Record Deals
Royalties
Album Release + Tour PR Campaign

A (brief) History of the Industry

1958–1995

In the vinyl and CD days, bands only started touring to promote the release of new music. The Record Labels would fund tours for their artist in hopes that people would buy the record. For 40 prosperous years, until the mid-1990's, many bands and labels took a ride down the record-selling money-highway.

1995 – 2010

The birth of the Internet brought radical changes to the music industry. In 1998, the DMCA, or Digital Millennium Copyright Act, was passed to aid the fight against music pirating. The DMCA "criminalized the technology or service intended to circumvent measures that protect copyrighted work."

Pirate Bay, Limewire, Transmission, uTorrent, Napster... These file sharing services altered the consumer mindset that they needed to pay for music at all. Fans were downloading millions of tracks at no cost from a wide range of artists through file-sharing platforms. And so Record Labels around the world ran out of money. They couldn't pay their artist to tour to sell records because no one was buying records.

The Record Companies, rather than re-invest in infrastructure that promoted a digital music marketplace, decided to fight back against tech companies and copyright infringers. By using the DMCA, they sued Internet service providers, tech companies, file-sharing services, and the people who used them. But these court cases were full of legal loopholes, time consuming legal procedure such as evidence gathering, and legal harassment of ordinary music listeners who had inconspicuously engaged in music file-sharing. Needless to say, these lawsuits weren't popular. Metallica and Dr. Dre both were involved in famous lawsuits against napster users after unreleased demos of their music were circulated without the group's knowledge and even played on commercial radio stations.

In 2001, the same year that the first iPod was released, everything changed. A Madonna single was leaked onto the web via Napster prior to its commercial release and the resulting court case finally brought down the file-sharing giant Napster, which at that point had a monthly user base of 26.4 Million users.

The mid-2000's were chaos for the music business. Each consecutive year the industry lost millions of dollars as the sale of vinyl, cassette tapes, and CDs plummeted.

Thanks to music pirating, there was a social disconnect between the consumption of music and paying for it; This is a problem that has persisted into today's music marketplace and is known as the *Value Gap*. The IFPI (International Federation of Phonographic Industries) identified 19.2 Million URL's as hosting infringing content and issued 336 Million takedown notices in 2016 alone.

There were a few notable exceptions: jam-bands, orchestra's, underground music, and Hip Hop. All of whom, for some reason or another, hadn't been interested in the Music Biz record-selling money-highway. Jam Bands and Orchestras built businesses based on concert revenue, Hip Hop was purposefully excluded, and Underground Music was by definition dissatisfied with the traditional music biz.

During this 15 year period, Music Industry Gross Revenue dropped nearly 40%. The birth of the Internet reset the playing the field for Record Companies and, for 15 years, the industry struggled to develop and invest in a digital music marketplace that was fair. More fair than their 40 years of success until 1998 and certainly more fair than the 15 that followed.

2010 – Present

In 2010, the music industry celebrated their first year of growth since 1995. By 2014, Music industry Wholesale revenue was approaching $5 Billion. The infrastructure for a digital music marketplace had finally been established.

2011:
1.8 Million Subscribers
9% of Total Music Industry Revenue

2014:
7.7 Paid Subscribers
27% of Total Music Industry Revenue

2017:
27 Million Paid Subscribers
51% of Total Music Industry Revenue

By the end of 2017, streaming services, such as Spotify, Pandora, YouTube Music, Google Play, and Apple Music reached 112 Million users. As a whole, the Recorded Music Industry revenue increased by 5.9% globally in 2017, the highest rate since 1997. Growth in streaming has more than offset 20% decline in digital downloads and a 7.6% decline in physical revenue that same year. Additionally, Streaming is driving growth in markets like China (20.3%), India (26.2%), and Mexico (23.6%). You can read more from the ***Global Music Report 2017***, published by the IFPI.

2019

Where do people discover new music?
- Word of mouth
- Soundcloud
- Spotify Discover weekly
- Music Festival Lineup
- Posters in Venues
- Physical Promotion
- In-Person music and file sharing
- Facebook Groups
- IG Story "Music"
- Snapchat Groups

Album Pre-Order

The most critical period for any product launch is the weeks and months leading up to the pre-order date — not the weeks and months following the product launch. When releasing an album, master the album at least 6 months earlier than your release date. These 6 months should be used to "shop" the album for press coverage, marketing, and promotion.

Examples include:
 - Sirius XM radio
 - College & Non-Commercial Radio
 - Spotify Playlist placement
 - Sync Licensing
 - Magazine & Blog coverage
 - Album reviews
 - Landing page traffic for re-targeting
 - Street team coordination

Pre-Order Exclusivity

Pre-Order Exclusivity gives you the opportunity listen to the album early with your fans, offer limited runs of merchandise and vinyl, and will give you upfront capital to cover some marketing, touring, or distribution expenses.

Your Album Pre-Order could include:
 - Album related merchandise (Lighter, Socks, T-Shirt)
 - Limited run of vinyl
 - Signed poster
 - Thank You Card
 - Access to an album listening party
 - Access to a Live-Stream Q&A with the Artist about the album

Record Labels

Record Label Departments:

A & R: Artist and Repertoire. Talent Scouting and overseeing artistic development of recording artists and songwriters. A&R also includes every activity of the artist up until the album release.

Sales: Retail. The Sales department works with record stores and music stores to put music on the shelves. Efforts are coordinated with the publicity and pr departments.

Marketing: Overall marketing plan for each album released by record label. Coordinates the plans of the sales and Promo departments.

Press/Publicity: Responsible for spreading the word about an artist or an album release. This department arranges articles to be written in newspapers and magazines, and handles all artist appearance on radio and television.

Graphics/Art: In charge of all artwork that goes into producing an album, such as cover art, advertisements, display graphics in stores, and tour posters.

Promotions: Main responsibility is to place each album released by record label on the radio.
Product Management

New Media: Social media management, Online marketing, music video production, streaming service

Production: Controls all aspects of the physical release of the album, such as CD and vinyl manufacturing and distribution.

Finance: Accounting department. Responsible for paying royalties

Business Affairs: Legal Department, responsible for all contracts made between the artist and the record label.

Types of Record Labels:

Major Labels
Universal, Sony, and Warner.

 – These Major Labels are known as the Big 3
 – They own the rights to an estimated 60% of the market share (sales) of the entire music catalog available for purchase (in the US).

Indie Labels
Sub Pop, 4AD, Sun, Matador, XL, JagJaguwar, and many more

 – Produce and distribute 66% of music titles but only account for 20% of market share (sales)
 – Some Independent Record Labels may sign distribution deals with Major Labels, allowing them to M& D their record more efficiently.
 – Major Labels sometimes partially or fully acquire an Independent Label.

Label Service Companies
A Label Services Company is paid by the artist to provide record label services. These services can be individual, such as vinyl pressing and distribution, or bundled similarly to a record deal. The artist will always retain ownership of their copyright and the label services company may take royalties from the artist depending on the monies paid to the label services company upfront.

For Example: You hire a label services company for:
 – Artwork
 – Vinyl pressing (500 units)
 – CD Manufacturing (3000 units)
 – Distribution
 – Shipping and Warehousing
 – Radio Promotion
 – Spotify Playlist promotion
 – Publicity

The Label Services company charges you:
    $45,000
    OR
    $20,000 + 20% of the royalties paid to the artist on the album

Music Distribution

The process of getting your music into the hands of your consumer is known as **distribution**. Manufacturing and Distribution companies will sign deals with the record label or artist for the rights to replicate and sell their music. The manufacturer/distributor takes a cut of the income, minus expenses, and returns the rest to the artist or label.

The Major Labels each own their own distributors. Before the era or Downloads, Music Distribution companies were the link between record labels and retail stores, such as record stores, Best Buy, Blockbuster, etc. In the 21st century, music distributors service their music to digital download and streaming platforms, such as iTunes, Spotify, and Pandora.

Physical Distributors

Receives the Master Recordings. CD and Vinyl Manufacturing. Physical Distributors will Manufacture a CD/Vinyl and distribute them. These companies have much larger storage, labor and shipping overhead costs than digital distro services. However, a revitalization of vinyl has revived a portion of this industry over the last 5 years. 2018 examples include:

- InGrooves
- Horus
- The Orchard
- CD Baby
- KinderCore

Digital Distribution

Service your music to digital download and streaming platforms. Digital Distributors are increasingly become one-stop-shops for royalty collection. Digital Distro typically take a commission from your royalties in exchange for their distribution, collecting, and accounting services. 2018 Examples include:

- CD Baby
- Tunecore
- Distrokid
- Loudr
- Ditto

Record Deals

Technically, a record deal is a "Recording License Agreement. The record label's purpose is to facilitate a license. The artist is the sound recording copyright holder and must assign rights to the record label. The artist and record label will then sign a **record deal** which entitles the label to control, distribute, promote, and exploit your record. Record deals are notoriously in favor of the label, but in many cases that is not true. At the end of the day, it depends on your bargaining position, negotiating skills, and relationship with the label.

Since there is no guarantee that any album or record release will be successful, Record Deals are drafted in such a way that the label is protected from the inherent financial risk, as well as to support their large organization.

Who owns the Master Recording?
The label will need a degree of legal control over your copyright to do their job. *"It is in the labels best interest to attain full ownership over the copyright for as long as possible."* As an artist, it is in your best interest to keep the copyright and license the rights for a short period of time. In most Major or Independent record deal, the label owns and controls the copyright to the master recording of the piece of music. In some Indie Deals and all Label Services company deals, the artist retains ownership of their master recordings. But in those deals, the artist either:
  – Has an immense amount of leverage over the record label
  – Owns their own label
  – Is expected to cover expenses related to the recording and releasing of the piece of music.

Record Label Advance:
A record label will almost always pay an artist a lump sum of monies upfront, known as an **advance**, against future artist royalties. This can be used any way that artist deems, such as a recording budget or to go on tour. The artist will not receive any royalties on their music until the entire advance has been paid back, or **recouped**, so its best to think of an advance as a line of credit rather than a pool of upfront cash. The advance is, however, non returnable.

So if the record label goes under you as the artist don't have to worry about paying that back.

Advances are also subject to **cross collateralization**, which means that if you don't recoup 100% of your advance on the first record, that debt is carried over onto the 2nd record. Similarly to the 3rd, and so on. For smaller, indie labels, the amount of the advance is highly negotiable, and as the artist I would recommend taking a smaller advance in exchange for a larger promotion budget for the album.

Royalties
Royalties are payments received in exchange for the use of intellectual property. The amount of royalty paid, except for Mechanical Royalties (*songwriters; more on that in the next chapter*), are negotiated as a part of the record deal. More importantly is the **Penny Rate**, which is the actual dollar amount the artist will receive after expenses from the sale of a record.

5 Types of Record Label Deal

360
A record deal between an artist and record label where the label receives a % of all of the artist's entertainment related revenue. "360" refers to the 360 degrees of control the record label has on your income streams. This includes Live Performance, Songwriting, Publishing, Merchandise, Sync Licensings, TV & Film Appearances, Lyric display, and Books. This deal is most common from Major Record labels and is highly unfavorable to the artist.

PPD – Published Price to Dealer
A record deal between an artist and record label that pays royalties based on the wholesale cost of the record.

SLRP – Suggested List Retail Profit
A record deal between an artist and record label that pays royalties based on the retail price of the record.

Profit Split

A record deal between an artist and record label that splits the net profits of the record 50/50. This deal is most common for indie record labels, or in situations where the owner of the master recording is also an owner of the record label. Just as the revenue is split 50/50, so are the expenses.

Label Services

A record deal between an artist and label services company. This record deal will include the terms of the services provided, such as manufacturing, distribution, marketing, artwork, or radio play. The artist always retains ownership of the master recording. In exchange, the label services company will take a % of revenue from the record. The amount of revenue is dependent on the upfront expenses paid by the artist to the label services company upfront.

M&D Deal – Manufacturing and Distribution

This is a negotiation between a record label, or owner of the master recording, and a distributor. In this deal, the distributor will manufacture physical copies of the record and distribute them in exchange for a % of record sales. This is especially good for small, indie record labels because it means they can print physical copies of their music without any upfront cost, which is significant for small labels on a tight budget. Similarly to an artist advance, the record label won't receive any money from those records sold until the manufacturing cost of the record is recouped.

Synchronization Deal

This is a negotiated per-title, non-exclusive deal between both the songwriter and performing artist and the producer of the audio-visual work. *Synchronization* refers to the marriage of audio and video into a new product. Sync deals are typically a flat fee upfront to both the songwriter and the performing artist in exchange for unlimited usage of the piece of music for a specified duration.

Record Deal Terms to know:

Exclusivity: Most record labels do not want to sign an artist for individual records. They will want long-term exclusivity over the artist to prevent them from moving to a larger record label and guarantee more material. If you are the artist, you should negotiate for option clauses.

Option Clause: Gives the record label the rights to release future records on the same terms as the initial deal, if the first release and collaboration is satisfactory to both the artist and the label.

In Perpetuity: "Forever". Many record labels will ask you to sign over your rights in perpetuity. Technically, this is impossible. If you are the artist, you need to change this language to better specify a duration of time.

Life of Copyright: For copyright's made after 1978, the life of the copyright is 70 years after the creator's death.

Release Commitment: A record deal clause that commits the label to releasing your record within 30–120 days after acceptance of the final product. It also grants you (the artist) the right to reclaim your recording copyright in case the record label does not release the record.

Statutory Rate: 9.1 cents per a 5 minute recording of music (in the US). This is the amount owed to the songwriter of a piece of music in the form of a mechanical royalty as determined by a specific group of United States judges known as the *rate court*.

Royalties

When an artist **records** a song, they are automatically granted 6 copyrights on the sound recording of that song, known as the *sound recording copyright*.

When an artist **writes** a song, meaning the lyrics and the melody, they are granted an additional set of rights, known as the *composition copyright*.

These 6 rights granted under copyright:
- Reproduce
- Make Derivative Work
- Display Publicly
- Perform Publicly
- Distribute
- Transmit Digitally

In order for a record label to release a record they need to have control over, or at least access to, these 6 copyrights. If an artist has signed a record deal, then the recording artist(s) must assign their copyright to the record label in exchange for royalties, which are called *artist royalties*.

The producer, or engineer, on the album also owns a piece of the copyright and so they, too, must be paid by the record label. These are called *producer royalties*.

Lastly, the writer of the melody and lyrics owns the composition copyright. Sometimes this is the same person but many times, especially in Country and Pop music, the song writer is not the same person who sings or records that song. This composition copyright is treated as a license instead of a transfer of ownership. The payment from the record label to the writer, or the composer, is called a *mechanical royalty*.

There are 3 additional royalties, or monies paid for the use of copyrighted work: *Public Performance*, *Sound Recording*, and *Sync*.

Artist Royalties

The Artist assigns the copyrights of the sound recording over to the record label in exchange for artist royalties. The Artist Royalty rate is negotiated in the record deal and recording contract.

 – Artist refers to the recording artist(s) of a piece of music.

Mechanical Royalty

Monies paid out to the writer, or composer, of a piece of music by the record label in exchange for using your intellectual property. This $ rate is determined by a US Court System, called the Rate Court, and payment for such a royalty is handled by the Harry Fox Agency, or HFA.

 – Composer refers to the person(s) responsible for writing the lyrics or melody of a piece of music.

Producer Royalty

Also known as Producer Points. Monies paid to the producer of a record, as stated in a recording contract. In most genres, the Producer royalty rate is 1–2%. In Hip Hop and electronic music, it can be as high as 50%.

 – The producer refers to the studio engineer(s) that "produces" the song into a physical form.

 – In Hip Hop, the Producer is the person(s) that creates the underlying Beat of the song.

 – This is different from the composer of electronic music.

Public Performance Royalty

Monies paid to the songwriter, or composer, of a piece of music any time your music is performed in public. The songwriter is owed a royalty when their song is played on terrestrial, satellite, and Internet radio, TV shows and commercials, or when it's performed in a live venue such as a club, restaurant, amusement park, or jukebox.

– Performing Rights Organization, or **PRO**, is an agency that collects the public performance royalty owed to songwriters and publishers.

 – In the United States, there are 3 PROs: BMI, ASCAP, and SESAC

Sound Recording Royalty

Monies paid only to the recording artist(s) of a piece of music. The sound recording royalty is similar to the Public Performance royalty, except that it goes to the performing artist of the song and not to the songwriter.

 – The Sound Recording royalty is only paid out when the piece of music is played on a non-interactive service, such as Pandora or a television show.

 – The Sound Recording Royalty is collected by a singular group in the United States known as SoundExchange. They hold onto all sound recording royalties owed until the owner comes forth to claim them.

Sync Royalty

Sync is short for Synchronization, or the process of "syncing" audio with video. Typically, a Sync Deal is a one-time flat fee paid up front for the unlimited use of that piece of music with a piece of video. In some cases however, It can come with a royalty payment known as a Sync royalty. The Sync Royalty is paid to both a music administrator, like the Harry Fox Agency, and to the record label or owner of the master recording. Both the performing artist and the songwriter are paid in a 50/50 split.

How Does the Royalty Money Flow?

Artist Royalty
Platform -> Digital Aggregator - > Record Label -> Artist

Mechanical Royalty
Platform -> Harry Fox Agency -> Publisher -> Songwriter

Producer Royalty
Platform -> Digital Aggregator -> Record Label -> Producer

Public Performance Royalty
User -> PRO -> Harry Fox Agency -> Publisher -> Songwriter

Sound Recording Royalty
Non-interactive Platform -> SoundExchange -> Artist

Sync Royalty
Multi-Media Producer -> Harry Fox Agency & Record Label -> Publisher & Artist (50/50)

Album Release & Tour Hypothetical PR Campaign

(Please note that for educational purposes I have chosen an excess of album release goals. When making a promo plan, or any sort of plan, you ought keep your goals within the realm of possibility.)

> **Strategic**
> **Timely**
> **Realistic**

Pre-Album Release Promo Goals
 - Create an invisible promo page on the website for anyone that is going to share your media
> *Editors, promoters, radio hosts, music directors, playlist curators*
 - Create 1 full length music video (live performance/in-studio) from the new record (album single).
 - Create 1 <60 promo video that highlights the album release
 - Upload mastered songs from the album to Sync Licensing websites

Pre-Tour Promo Goals
 - Album supported Tour Dates updated onto your Spotify Account
 - Facebook Event "landing pages" created for each show + market
 - Updated City Event Calendars in each market
 - Updated EventBrite/BandsInTown directory for each tour date
 - Street Team Coordination for target markets
> 1-5 people on the ground for distributing physical promo
> 10-100 people online distributing digital promo

PR Goals
 - Album Feature/Coverage in 5 National Music Magazines
 - Album Reviews in 5 Digital Blogs
 - Album "Single" played on:
> 20 college radio stations
> 15 non-commercial radio stations.
> 5 Actively curated Spotify Playlists
 - Instagram/Snapchat story takeover's prepared for each market
> These can be with the venues, other artists on the bill, or even Ticket Giveaway winners.

Advertising Content Creation

1 Short Promo video
- This promo video should be less than 15 seconds and prepared vertically for Instagram/Snapchat Story Advertising.
- This will be day-of-show advertising only, using geo-targeting to advertise to an audience within a geographical distance from the venue

2 Unique photo + text Combinations
- These are for Facebook advertisements
- Make them general for the whole tour, or dial them into specific markets that you need to improve or want to sell more tickets in.
- Focus on strong headlines
- You should make 2 of these ads to A/B test their efficiency when reviewing your analytics

> **A/B Testing**: is a randomized experiment with 2 variants. In Advertising, split testing lets you compare your advertisements against each other to determine effectiveness.

1 <60 promo video
- Prepare this video for Facebook (landscape) & Instagram (square).
- The promo video should promote awareness for the performance and showcase your music
- You should use this video to target towards a Cold Audience and spread awareness about the show. Make sure that you are leading to the Facebook Event page and not a ticket link!

** If your advertising budgets are prepared ahead of time, the venue may cover this cost under their marketing expenses in your contract.

6 Months Before Album Release

Written Press

- Write a Press Release announcing the record/tour
- Gather a list of weeklies/bi-weeklies and any local news outlets in the markets you are playing on the album release tour
- Write the first editorial pitch to send to music magazines and blogs that would be interested in the record.
  > *This could be an Interview with the band, an exclusive pre-listen, single leak, or album review.*

Radio Promo

- Hire a Radio PR team to push your record to college and non-profit community radio stations
OR
- Do It Yourself. Gather a list of stations and DJ's that might want to spin your record. Be diligent in collecting accurate information and only choose DJ's that would be interested in playing your music.

Social Media

- Begin Planning a Live-In-Studio-Stream of the album to Facebook, Instagram, YouTube, or other live streaming platforms.
- Plan a Q&A session with the band to discuss the album and announce it to your audience so they can prepare questions.
- You can recycle this content into an interview pitch to editorials later in the PR campaign.

Touring

- Hire a graphic designer to complete the Tour Poster, Album Artwork, advertising materials, and any other design work you may need

4 Months Before

- All written press and video promo material should be finished
- Discuss which markets will receive the most attention for your advertising and marketing efforts.
- Finalize album release budgets and tour budgeting
- Confirm dates and holds on the tour
    Challenge any existing holds that help route you to more $$$
- Begin building your Tour Budget

3 Months Before Album Release

- Write an editorial pitch offering the exclusive release and coverage of the album single
- Open up album pre-sales to the public to bring in some revenue and help offset your marketing expenses
- Announce the tour
- Create FB specific Event pages for each show on the tour to be used as landing pages for your marketing efforts
- Double check that all ticket purchase links are accurate and working
- Update your merchandise to reflect the album pre-sale and any new merchandise

2 Months Before

- Write and send an editorial pitch with early access to the album and ask the publication for an album review.
- Write the scripts and begin audio, photo or video production for:
    Facebook marketing
    Instagram marketing
    IG and Snapchat story marketing
    Email newsletter marketing
- Advance with every venue to confirm Performance Contracts, Hospitality and Technical Riders.

- Confirm with the venue what responsibility they will take for promotion and marketing the show; discuss marketing opportunities.

> *Share with them your marketing plan and make sure they have all the necessary ad-mats to promote the show.*

- Begin coordinate a Street Team in markets that you want to build.

1 Month Before

- Coordinate In-Studio performances or interviews alongside your tour
  > *Emphasize College Radio stations*
- Activate your Street Team members to begin spreading physical promotion and posters
- Create a finalized plan for digital advertising in each market while you are on the road that emphasizes show awareness and ticket giveaways.

Release Day!

- Play the best, most memorable show of your career!
- Include Special guests, costumes, theatrics, giveaways, etc. Make this a show to remember
- Get some sleep and pack a bag.

If the record is good, word will spread.
So take a day off and get ready to literally take your show on the road.

TERMINOLOGY

Music Industry Terms to Know

Music Industry Terms to Know

Advancing the Show: Confirming in advance the details surrounding your show with he venue or promoter.

Artist Royalties: The Artist assigns the copyrights of the sound recording over to the record label in exchange for artist royalties. The Artist Royalty rate is negotiated in the record deal and recording contract.

Auto-Responder: An Automated bot or program used for confirming email sign-up forms. It will send an initial email to a patron thanking them for signing up for the newsletter, visiting the website, or purchasing a product.

Bounce: A bounce is when a visitor comes to a page, but doesn't interact with the page in any way and then leaves. Essentially, people are coming to your site and either finding what they want but not anything else or not finding what they want at all.

Brand: Promise of Quality and Consistency

Buy On: Is when a smaller artist pays to be the supporting act for a larger artist.

Buy Out: Is when, in lieu of providing a meal to the band, the venue will just pay a flat sum to the band to purchase food.

Challenge: A booking agent with a 2nd Hold may *Challenge* an agent with a 1st hold for a date at a venue if they are ready to commit to a contract. Upon being issued a Challenge, the promoter of the show will give the agent with a 1st hold the option of committing or backing out.

Contact Information: Should always include Phone number, and Email

Conversion Tracking Pixel: A single line of code that keeps track of actions performed by your audience via Google Adwords or Facebook Ads manager. These actions include clicking on a button, signing up for a newsletter, completing a purchase, or visiting your website.

Copy: Written material, in contrast to photo or video.

CPC: Cost Per Click Advertising. An advertising model used to direct traffic to websites, in which an advertiser pays a publisher when the ad is clicked. Pay-per-click is commonly associated with first-tier search engines, such as Google.

Current Press: A display of press coverage, reviews, interviews, any and all mention of your work. "3rd party endorsements are by far more powerful than anything you can say about yourself and your work"

Dead Wood: Unsold Tickets

Discography: A list of publicly available recordings. Your band's discography should be located somewhere on the website with links to the music if it's available

Door Deal: A % of the money made at the door via Ticket Sales. Embargo: Typically a period of time when you are not allowed to say or publish anything around a story or piece of news. Examples include a surprise album release or a festival lineup.

Gate Keepers: A person who controls access to something. Gatekeepers in the music industry include: Music Directors at Radio Stations, Arts and Culture section Editors at Magazines, Booking Agents, Talent Buyers. These are people that you need to impress to attain a goal in the music biz.

Guarantee: Flat Fee that is Guaranteed to the artist no matter the venue income or expenses related to the show.

Hall Fees: A percentage of the total merch sales taken by the venue in exchange for allowing merchandise to be sold. Typically 20–25%. Larger rooms only, like Theaters, Festivals, and maybe some Large Clubs. A Hall Fee may be negotiated out of a contract in exchange for a smaller Guarantee.

Hard Ticket: Is an event where the main attraction is a specific artist. People in attendance are only paying to see a specific artist(s). Hard Ticket example: Headlining or Support artist in a club or theatre.

Hold: If an agent wants to book a date at a venue to perform, they can "hold" the date before committing to the show. If another Agent wants the date, they can get a "2nd Hold", or a "3rd Hold", and so on. In–House: Staff within a company or organization responsible for public relations function

Keyword: Keywords are the words and phrases that people are searching for in search engines (i.e. Google) to get to your site. Keywords are generally the most responsible for generating website traffic.

Label Services Company: A type of record label that is paid to provide record label services to the artist. These services can be individual, such as vinyl pressing and distribution, or bundled similarly to a record deal.

Lead Magnet: A free resource that your audience perceive as valuable enough to submit their personal details in return for it.

List–Serve: An electronic mailing list

Macro Content: Long Form, high cost content. Examples include: Blog Posts, Photo Galleries, You– tube Videos, Documentaries, Podcasts, & Live Streams.

Main Contact: Manager or Band Leader. Someone to answer the phone for business matters.

Mechanical Royalty: Monies paid out to the writer, or composer, of a piece of music by the record label in exchange for using your intellectual property. This $ rate is determined by a US Court System, called the Rate Court, and payment for such a royalty is handled by the Harry Fox Agency, or HFA.

Micro Content: Short form, low cost content. Examples include: Photos, Videos less than 60 seconds, Text, Most Social Media Posts.

Negative Keywords: In pay per click advertising, negative keywords prevent advertisements from displaying for particular keyword phrases.

Newsletter: A regular release of new information pertinent to the attraction and interest of registered patrons.

One Sheet: Condenses all the aspects of a Press Kit into one page; traditionally used to promote an album.

Papering the House: Is when the venue gives away tickets to a show in order to make the room look full. This is usually not announced to the band until it is time to settle the show.

Penny Rate: The actual dollar amount the artist will receive after expenses from the sale of a record

Point of Contact: The Venue Manager, Production Manager, Promoter, Talent Buyer, or any person that can confirm details about the show on behalf of the venue.

Press Release: Written information th is deemed to be newsworthy. Often sent out to journalists and/ or interested parties. A reference for writers on a particular story. Informational writing.

Promo Videos: Either videos of performances or promotional videos that showcase an upcoming release.

Radius Clause: A time frame or geographic restriction that prevents an artist from playing a competing show. Standard radius Clause is 60 Days and 60 Miles. It gives the promoter a form of territorial exclusivity over the performance.

Rider: Document attached to (rides) the performance contract detailing important information about an artists hospitality or technical needs.

Runner: A person or persons hired to act as personal shopper or driver for the band and crew

SEO: Search Engine Optimization. (Check out Ubersuggest.com)

Settlement: The process where the Promoter of the show/Venue Owner goes through an itemized list of income and expenses with the Artist and then pays out the remaining balance.

Social Media: The implementation, discussion, and execution of a Social multimedia platform, long term goals for client-customer dialogue, and brand image awareness through social media.

Soft Ticket: An event where the event itself is the main attraction and ticket seller and the artists are apart of the event. Soft Ticket example: City Music and Arts Festival

Split Point: All revenues from the Box Office - Tax - Expenses - Artist Guarantee = The Split Point. If you reach the Split Point, that is called "going into Points". Any overage past the Split point is then split per a previously negotiated Percentage.

Split-Testing (A/B): A randomized experiment with 2 variants. In Advertising, split testing lets you compare your advertisements against each other to determine effectiveness.

Stage Plot: A Stage Plot is a list of Inputs, Outputs, and Stage directions for the venue production staff. Your stage plot should include: *Instruments, Amp Type, Power Needed, Mics needed, A full and accurate I/O (Input / Output list), & Preference on Stage Position (diagram)*

Street Team: The Marketing term for a group of people that "hit the streets" to promote an event or a product.

Talent Buyer: Hires the artist to play at venues. The Talent Buyer takes the most risk and has the most upside. They are paid a negotiated % of the show's net profit and work directly with the Booking Agent

Traffic: The user data sent and received by your website. Generally, it is the number of users and the numbers of pages they visit.

Underplay: A show that is guaranteed to sell-out because the venue capacity is so much smaller than the expected attendance

Value Gap: The growing mismatch between the value that user upload services, such as YouTube, extract from music and the revenue returned to those who create and invest in music.

Vs Deal: Flat Fee VS Door Deal, whichever is higher in favor of the artist.

Website: The Main hub for all your Professional Musical activity.

The End!

Words cannot express how happy I am to see you at the end of this book. Thank you for taking the time to read and learn from me. Please use this information to absolutely crush 2019 and bring your musical dreams to fruition.

I added little bits of my personal experiences and humor throughout its pages. This book is my first attempt at creating a practical guide for navigating the industry in 2019, especially for youngsters in the biz. Any and all feedback is greatly appreciated!

Please, email me at JosiahGarrettMusic@gmail.com

Or, we can connect on social media! I'm on Facebook, linkedIn, Instagram, and YouTube!

You are awesome, and I appreciate you.

Peace!
~Josiah Garrett
(Author, Bass Player, Entrepreneur, Educator)